THE CHILDCARE BIBLE

The ultimate guide to all forms of childcare

LUCY MARTIN

Vermilion
LONDON

1 3 5 7 9 10 8 6 4 2

Published in 2009 by Vermilion, an imprint of Ebury Publishing

Ebury Publishing is a Random House Group company

The Random House Group Limited Reg. No. 954009

Addresses for companies within the Random House Group can be found at www.rbooks.co.uk

A CIP catalogue record for this book is available from the British Library

The Random House Group Limited supports The Forest Stewardship Council (FSC), the leading international forest certification organisation. All our titles that are printed on Greenpeace approved FSC certified paper carry the FSC logo. Our paper procurement policy can be found at www.rbooks.co.uk/environment

Printed and bound in Great Britain by Clays Ltd, St Ives Plc

ISBN 9780091924263

For more information on childcare and the author, please visit www.childcarebible.co.uk

This book is a work of non-fiction. The names of people in the case studies have been changed solely to protect the privacy of others.

For my children – Stephanie, Gina and Jude – and everyone who has played a part in caring for them, including their grandparents; our nannies Katie, Cara and Natalie; our favourite babysitter Joe; my brother/after-school carer Richard 'Uncle Dick'; and my very supportive husband Richard

Contents

Acknowledgements ix

Introduction 1

Chapter 1 The Decision to Go Back to Work 11
Chapter 2 The Right Childcare for Your Family 21
Chapter 3 Maternity Nurses, Doulas, Night Nannies and Mothers' Helps 41
Chapter 4 Nannies 61
Chapter 5 Nannyshares 123
Chapter 6 Au Pairs and Babysitters 145
Chapter 7 Childminders 181
Chapter 8 Day Nurseries, Workplace Childcare and Children's Centres 203
Chapter 9 Nursery Schools, Playgroups and School-based Care 229
Chapter 10 Using Relatives 249
Chapter 11 From the Horse's Mouth: Parents' Experiences and Top Tips 263

Conclusion Where to Go from Here . . . 281

Appendix 1 Contracts of Employment 283
Appendix 2 Finances 293
Appendix 3 Children with Special Needs 301
Appendix 4 List of EEA Countries 305
Appendix 5 Childcare Qualifications 307

Resources 313
Index 333

Acknowledgements

I would especially like to thank the employment team at Speechly Bircham for their time and effort in contributing to the legal aspects of this publication.

I would also like to thank my children for telling me exactly what they thought of their own childcare experiences, and all of my contributors (too numerous to list here), who helped complete the picture. Thanks also to my agent, Amanda Preston, and Julia Kellaway, my very capable editor.

Introduction

The last century has seen a multitude of changes in the way Britain works, and in the way Britons work. A hundred years ago the concept of two middle-class working parents was almost unheard of, but during the war years of the 20th century and beyond, women have proved themselves capable of taking on what men have long been managing single-handed: the hunting and gathering side of raising a family. Today it is universally acknowledged that providing for the family is not the exclusive domain of the male partner, and although many women stay at home during the early months or years of motherhood, a staggering 89 per cent of them eventually return to paid work, and need to find childcare.

Supported by legislation and their own reputation as conscientious and reliable employees, women continue to defy the tradition that mummy = stay-at-home. Outperforming boys at school, high-achieving girls are taking their skills to the marketplace. Increasing numbers of women are setting up their own businesses, and aside from the economic benefits of working, the personal-fulfilment aspect is becoming less of a taboo. Many more women are finding that maintaining their pre-childbearing identity gives them the enthusiasm and freshness they need to feel fulfilled as mothers.

The emancipation of women has come far, but there is still a long road ahead. A mother choosing to go back to work still faces a number of barriers before she even tackles the childcare issue. The dip in self-esteem following childbirth can lead her to doubt herself as a professional career woman. She is also likely during maternity leave to have taken on a raft of new household responsibilities, simply by spending time at home. Shopping, meal-planning, organising holidays and taking the car to the mechanic all fall under the remit of whichever partner is at home. Shaking off those responsibilities, throwing them back into the pot to be shared out again equally, is a step a new mother may not naturally take, and her decision to go back to the office will depend on whether she can cope with a job as well as masterminding everything on the home front. Add to this social and peer pressure to stay at home, and the struggle to make the decision becomes, for some, too difficult to address.

One reason mothers cite for their decision not to use childcare is that 'Nobody will love your child more than you do.' But does your child's carer need to love him or her as much as you do? It is highly likely she will love children, enjoy looking after them, be trained, qualified, possibly registered and certainly experienced in their care (unlike most first-time mothers). Looking at what she can give your child, rather than the one thing (motherhood) she can't, is the first step to escaping the spiral of negative thinking. In fact, many nannies come to love the children they look after, and may be heartbroken when they leave a job. Most good nanny–family relationships continue way beyond the years that the nanny is employed professionally – precisely because she and the children have developed such a strong bond.

If you can't bear the thought of handing over your children to someone else, and can afford not to work, then your choice is made for you. Other women have no alternative other than to go back. Antonia is a mother of three, who has been single since her husband left just after the third was born: 'When you're on your own and you need to work, you have no choice but to let other people into the scenario. My children have all sorts of proxy mummies and daddies who have helped look after them over the years, and they still love them all!'

Grandparents might be the ideal option, but today families are often scattered geographically. Many women have babies later in life, so their own parents are less likely to be fit for full-time nannying; and those who are may prefer to fill their retirement with new experiences or foreign travel, and to enjoy their grandchildren as an occasional treat.

The media both eulogise and denigrate the childcare scenario. A recent Cambridge University study into the influence of working mothers on family life showed that more than half of men *and* women think that a family will suffer if a mother is in full-time employment. The same study showed that this wasn't the result of a conservative backlash: there was also a significant decrease in the proportion of men and women who believed that the man should go out to work while the woman looked after the children.

For more than 30 years 'evidence' has been building to indicate that preschool children who spend long hours in daycare are more likely to display aggression and disobedience than those who stay at home or attend part-time. A recent study even found that this antisocial behaviour may even be contagious – showing that the media hype around childcare is becoming almost as powerful as that around passive smoking. The studies continually fail to address the many variables that affect the results.

Over the years, Ofsted reports have been splashed across the media whenever a childcare provider has had a less than impressive rating. Overall, however, the standard of registered childcare across the country is improving, and the number of childcare settings rated 'inadequate' is decreasing. Child-minders commenting on ratings which fall short are at pains to point out that a high rating is, to a great extent, dependent on the production of outstanding plans, observations and records rather than the amount of quality time spent with the children.

It's not just social pressure and the media that get in the way. Practical obstacles exist too. Some mothers cite cost as the reason they haven't gone back to work: 'It's just not financially worthwhile . . .' As the proprietor of a nanny agency, I am the last person to suggest that childcare is cheap. To pay a qualified and experienced full-time live-out nanny in London, inclusive of tax and National Insurance contributions, means deducting £40,000 from your gross salary. Elsewhere in the country, costs can be a lot lower – in Scotland and the north of England, for example, a full-time live-out nanny's gross salary will be more like £22,000. However, nannies in some areas in Cheshire and the south west of England charge rates not that dissimilar to London. Clare Riley runs a nanny agency in Manchester: 'People expect to pay less outside London,' she says, 'but we are in a pocket of "wealth" here which means effectively that nannies can and do charge top rates.'

But there are less expensive options: a childminder in the south east can cost as little as £150 per week (the national average being £127), and a place in a Sure Start children's centre even less. Current government policy provides for free childcare places for three- to four-year-olds at all nurseries, and most employers offer a salary-sacrifice scheme to help their employees pay for childcare.

Legislation has also brought welcome changes in part-time and flexible working. Twenty years ago combining work and family was a distant dream for many, but in recent years women (and men) have been more open and vocal about their desire for a satisfying work–life balance, and more successful in finding it.

Demographic changes have played a big part in this. In 2007 there were more first-time mothers aged 30–34 than 25–29. Research suggests that the trend towards later maternity is strongest among women with better educational qualifications, with some postponing childrearing to pursue their careers. That means the typical employee who asks to work flexibly so that she can combine career and family is more senior, has more expertise and will be more difficult to replace. Employers are also recognising the commercial argument for retaining mothers in the workplace. Mothers who combine work and family:

- tend to have a well-developed ability to prioritise
- are totally focused on getting the job done within the allotted time frame (if you have to leave at 5.30 p.m. to pick up the children you will not be sidetracked)
- are far less political than their male counterparts

Plenty of parents use childcare even if both don't go out to work – most commonly mothers' helps and au pairs. Some mothers never go back after having a child; with the arrival of a second or third, others find the combination of parental responsibilities and a demanding job too much. The use of childcare by those who don't work carries an unjustified social stigma, but 60 per cent of families with a parent at home still do it. You may use childcare without working for a number of reasons:

- you have a newborn baby and are exhausted
- you have several children and can't be in three places at once
- you want to spend time doing something for yourself
- you want time to work on a business idea
- you want to study, get training or pursue a hobby
- a family member has a disability
- you have caring responsibilities for another family member
- it makes you more effective as a parent/homemaker
- you just need extra help

There is still a bit of a wow factor about mums who manage everything related to home and children on their own – I admire Denise, a mum who, alongside working as a classroom assistant at our children's school, cooks hearty casseroles and traditional puddings every day, keeps her house immaculate and is rarely to be seen out of her running gear on days off. Even today there is huge pressure on a woman to be a domestic goddess, but accepting that you're not one is the first step to real fulfilment. There is a compromise to be made here: all of the women I spoke to while I was researching this book confirmed my suspicions. Your family probably won't notice that the shirts were ironed, the socks put away or groceries bought by a third party, you will be much better company if you've spent your day on something more personally fulfilling. As Jessica, mother of three boisterous boys in Edinburgh, said, 'I'd be wandering the streets in pyjamas if I didn't have some form of childcare . . .'

So you need childcare, but where do you start? There may have been a welcome revolution in the way childcare in Britain is supported and organised, but it doesn't make the headlines, and you don't have to grapple with it until you become a parent, which is when you have neither the time nor the energy to unravel and understand the system. The advent of Sure Start, which aims to improve early-years childcare provision, and the increasing power of Ofsted, may have brought increased regulation to the market but has inevitably led to consumer confusion. You might hear on the grapevine about tax credits for low-income families and a voucher scheme for employers to pay childcarers direct, 'But where the hell do I get these vouchers?' one exasperated mother asked me recently. The plethora of websites that has sprung up around the childcare market only increases that confusion – government booklets and agency leaflets, though well intentioned, simply don't offer a comprehensive enough package for the modern parent.

I wrote this book, first, because it *is* the comprehensive information resource that was missing when I was looking for childcare. When I had my first baby I had no idea where to start the search or even what it was I wanted. Like many parents, I relied on word of mouth, bits and pieces I picked up from magazines, and the experiences of friends and colleagues when it came to making choices about nurseries and nannies. My understanding of the options available was ill-informed, my decisions, looking back, often wrong. I wish now that my expectations had been managed better – if only someone had told me how often little babies are excluded from nursery through illness, or that you should start looking for a nanny three months before you need one. Knowing nothing about interviewing nannies, I lost out on great candidates and missed warning signs in others. It was a case of trial and error, until my most successful childcare arrangement arrived entirely by chance in the form of wrap-around care at the local state primary school.

The second reason I wanted to write this book was to empower women to return to work by offering real and practical solutions to typical childcare dilemmas, particularly cost. I have met mothers who assumed that a nanny would be too expensive and whose employers lost out on valuable talent: they hadn't heard of nannysharing. I have met employers who consider mothers a bad investment because of the time they take off to look after sick children. They hadn't heard of Emergency Childcare – a service that firms are buying into across the UK, supplying temporary nannies to families of employees if the existing nanny is ill or the child is ill and cannot attend nursery. Mothers also tend to deduct the cost of childcare from their own salaries when they decide whether or not to go back to work – as if childcare wasn't a shared responsibility . . .

What I hope I have achieved with this book is clarity and completeness. I wanted to create the essential companion for every working parent, and I have interviewed parents across the country to be as inclusive and broad as possible in my approach. I have covered all the basic forms of childcare provision available in the UK, showing how to assess the facilities and staff, what to ask and how to work out if it's for you. With checklists and case studies, I set out the pros and cons of every option, straight from the horse's mouth (or the horse's parents anyway); and in a real departure from other sources of information on childcare, I have included important legal aspects of returning to work, what you can expect from your employer, and the nitty-gritty of being an employer yourself. As a mother, and having used most types of childcare, I have the personal experience that adds value to any handbook that aims to teach.

This book is for all parents, but if I speak to you as a mother, please understand that this is because, in my many years of running a nanny agency, only a handful of my thousand or so clients have been men, and women tend to plan the childcare because they are off work at the relevant time. I would, however, like to encourage more men to get involved. I hope that the accessibility of the book will result in a higher number of parents sharing the responsibility.

HOW TO USE THIS BOOK

The book is divided into chapters that relate to different types of childcare, starting with a summary overview. I have started with maternity nurses and possibilities for the early days with a baby, moved to nannies and nannyshares, then childminders, nurseries and nursery schools, finishing with a chapter on the dubiously named 'relative care'. I would advise everyone to read Chapters 1 and 2; then, if you are certain about what you want, go to the relevant chapter (using the chart on pages 26–7). If you are not certain, or simply want to know everything there is to know before you make a decision, read every chapter, and don't forget to look at the case studies in 'From the Horse's Mouth' at the end of the book, which give you some real-life experiences that may influence the decisions you finally make.

There are regional differences in salaries, fees and registration requirements, particularly if you live in Scotland, Wales or Northern Ireland, but I have tried to give an idea of those variations wherever relevant. Regulatory aspects also vary from region to region – whereas registered childcare settings (nurseries, nursery schools, playgroups and childminders) are inspected by Ofsted in England, in Wales this will be the Care Standards Inspectorate for Wales, in Scotland the Scottish Commission for the Regulation of Care, and in Northern Ireland a Health and Social Services Board or Trust.

Alongside the book, the website www.childcarebible.co.uk provides legal and technical updates that are too fast-changing to include in this book.

I hope that you enjoy reading this book as much as I have enjoyed putting it together.

CHAPTER 1

The Decision to Go Back to Work

The starting point for most parents, before they even look at the question of childcare, is the whole issue of going back to work. Are you going to go back to work? If so, when and how? It is only after you have established the answers to these three questions that you can begin to decide what kind of care is right for your child, as well as when and where to start looking.

TO BE OR NOT TO BE A WORKING PARENT

Making the decision to go back to work is no simple task. Although many women feel certain of their intentions one way or the other before they embark on maternity leave, the arrival of the baby can trigger unexpected emotions that sit uncomfortably with the notion of picking up the reins where you left off.

Your own feelings about it will be particular to you, and are as valid as the next person's. The important thing is to consider what you really want (regardless of what you think is expected of you) and to plan your return to work around that personal mission. You may be surprised at where your gut feeling takes you.

Your employer may pressure you to say at a very early stage whether or not you intend to come back. You will understand that business need, but you can still keep your options and the lines of communication open: this may give you the opportunity to tailor-make a job to return to, particularly if your current position requires a lot of travel or antisocial hours.

We have all read stories in the press about high-powered mothers getting back to their desks within hours of giving birth, but this is unusual outside the US. In the UK we have a relatively generous entitlement to maternity leave. Some mothers don't take the whole lot – they say they would never go back if they stayed off work for a year. Others believe it's too long to be out of the marketplace. Melanie, an associate at an accountancy firm in Manchester, says: 'We all know we can take up to a year off, but that would be an unfeasible amount of time to be out of the office and still expect to stay on top of things. When I had my first baby, I went back after six months and it was hard leaving him at such an early age, but I had to weigh that up with the amount of catch-up I'd be doing otherwise. It seems to be all about sacrifices at first, but the good news is you get used to being back very quickly, and once your childcare is working, that takes a great weight off your mind.' It varies according to the type of job you have and what kind of maternity package you have been offered. It is common among banks and City institutions to offer an incentive to mothers to come back early, but beware the policy that asks for all the money you have been paid to be returned if you stay fewer than six months – they will be perfectly within their rights to ask for it if that's what it says in the contract.

PRACTICAL ADVICE ON RETURNING TO WORK

If you're going back to work after having children, start to plan your return early in your maternity leave. Feel free to keep your thoughts to yourself and be flexible: your views may change as your baby grows. If you are self-employed you will need to put your own measures in place to deal with your absence. If you are employed, this will be up to your employer. A number of practical and legal questions will influence your decisions about childcare. Here are some of the most commonly asked.

WHEN DO YOU HAVE TO TELL THEM WHETHER OR NOT YOU'RE COMING BACK?

If you have decided not to return to work, you must give your employer the notice period specified in your contract of employment, in the same way as you would if you had decided to leave for any other reason. If you do not have a contract, or your contract says nothing about the notice period, in most cases you would need to give one week's notice. If you are on one month's contractual notice, let your employer know a month before the end of your maternity leave that you are not coming back. If you do this at least a month before your maternity leave is due to end you will not need to return to work out your notice period. If you don't tell your employer in time, you may be required to return to work for whatever is left of your notice period. In most cases, however, an employer is unlikely to insist on this.

If you refuse to return to work without having given the required notice then, strictly speaking, your employer will have a claim against you. You have broken the contract and your employer is entitled to be compensated by you for the loss caused by that breach. In most situations, though, it will be hard to prove any loss, and your employer probably won't find it worth spending time, energy and money on pursuing you.

If you wish to return to work and plan to return at the point when your full statutory maternity leave expires, you do not need to notify your employer. The law requires them to assume that you will return at that point. If you wish to go back to work earlier than the end of your statutory maternity leave entitlement, you will need to give your employer at least eight weeks' notice of your return date. If you do not, your employer may delay it. If you have informed your employer of your early-return date, then wish to change it, you can bring it forward or delay it (but not past the end of your maternity leave). You must simply notify your employer at least eight weeks before your original return date.

CAN THEY SACK YOU WHILE YOU'RE ON MATERNITY LEAVE?

Yes, as long as the dismissal is for a fair reason that is not linked to your pregnancy. For example, you can lawfully be made redundant while on maternity leave where a genuine redundancy situation exists and you are selected on fair, objective and non-discriminatory grounds that are not pregnancy-related. If your job becomes redundant during your maternity leave, your employer is obliged to look for an alternative role for you.

If, however, you are dismissed for a reason connected with your pregnancy or statutory maternity leave, this is classed automatically as unfair dismissal. It is unlawful discrimination on the ground of your pregnancy, with no limit on the amount of loss you are able to recover. Most employers are very reluctant to dismiss employees who are on maternity leave or who are about to go on maternity leave or who have recently returned from maternity leave. If it happens to you, or you think it may be about to happen, consult a solicitor as soon as possible.

WHAT IS YOUR ENTITLEMENT TO A PAY RISE WHILE YOU'RE ON MATERNITY LEAVE?

While on maternity leave you are entitled to receive salary increases in line with any that would have applied if you had not taken maternity leave.

PARENTAL LEAVE

If you're a working parent, you can take up to 13 weeks' parental leave for each child before their fifth birthday (more if you have a disabled child). Your employer doesn't have to pay you when you take this leave, but they might as part of your employment package.

FLEXIBLE AND PART-TIME WORKING

Flexible working is becoming a popular choice among parents who want to get the balance right between work and family. Whether or not to request it will be your decision. It amounts to asking your employer for a new working pattern to help you care for your child.

Legally, both men and women have rights regarding flexible working. All parents with children under the age of six (or a disabled child under 18) have the right to request to work flexibly, but you must:

- have worked for your employer for at least 26 weeks
- be the child's mother, father, adopter, legal guardian, foster-parent or the partner of one of these
- have responsibility for the child's upbringing
- be making the application so that you'll be able to care for the child

'Flexible working' describes any working pattern adapted to suit your needs. Common types of flexible working are:

- part-time: working fewer than the normal hours, perhaps by working fewer days per week
- flexi-time: choosing when to work (there's usually a core period during which you must work)
- annualised hours: you have a specific number of hours per year that you need to work, usually some being set and others down to your choice
- compressed hours: working your agreed hours over fewer days
- staggered hours: different start, break and finish times for employees in the same workplace
- jobsharing: sharing a job designed for one person with someone else
- homeworking: working from home

You can combine any of these working patterns to come up with something to suit your circumstances. Remember that if you are doing less work for your employer, your pay will be reduced accordingly.

Some mothers are happy to go back full-time after the first child, but change their mind with the arrival of the second.

> ***Philippa*** *had her second baby when the first child was five. She assumed she would go back to work full-time as she had with her elder child, but the reality of being a family of four made her see things differently. 'I felt as if our family was complete. Having two children seemed to throw everything into sharp relief and I just knew I couldn't go back full-time again.' Luckily her years of loyalty paid off and she took her high-flying position down from five to three days a week.*

HELP WITH FINANCING CHILDCARE

Government taxation policy in recent years has been focused on helping the poorest families and, in particular, enabling mothers to return to work. Tax credits and childcare vouchers are just two of the incentives launched to achieve this aim. Technically, all employers could be signing up to the childcare-vouchers scheme, which operates as a salary sacrifice: the company makes a contribution on the employee's behalf for registered childcare costs out of the employee's gross salary. The voucher scheme applies to all forms of registered childcare – nurseries, registered childminders and registered nannies. See the website for full details on how the schemes work and whether you qualify.

MAKE THE MOST OF COMMUNICATIONS TECHNOLOGY: HOMEWORKING

The Internet and mobile phones have revolutionised work and leisure, and brought the two closer together. Nearly everyone has a home Internet connection and a mobile phone, and an increasing number of us have BlackBerrys. We no longer expect that when we communicate with someone else in another company, or even in our own, that they will be sitting at a desk five days a week, from nine till five. Flexible working is becoming a practical everyday reality. You can stay in touch with your contacts and team almost as easily outside the office as you can in it.

TALKING TO THE HR DEPARTMENT

If you throw all the above factors into the mix you will see that it makes commercial sense for companies to embrace and develop flexible working practices for their working parents. Your HR department will probably be well versed on the commercial reasons for flexible working as a concept, but in case you need to help them construct the argument for your own flexible-working request, here, in HR speak, are the five top reasons why they should embrace it:

Engagement Better employee engagement is the *raison d'être* of every HR team across the world

Retention The mother who has found a way to combine work and family is less likely to leave

Recruitment If an employer is recruiting people of a certain age and level, those recruits are more likely to look at the family policies they have in place

Absenteeism Working from home reduces levels of absenteeism in the firm

Diversity Encouraging engagement from working fathers, as well as working mothers, will go a long way to helping employers achieve their diversity targets

Other things you could reasonably expect and/or request from your employer are:

- extended maternity leave
- training courses specifically aimed at helping you combine work and family
- back-up childcare provision (see Chapter 3 page 41 on temporary childcare)
- an advice and support telephone line specifically aimed at working parents
- Special Carer days

CHAPTER 2

The Right Childcare for Your Family

WHAT KIND OF FAMILY ARE YOU?

Every family is different, and the sort of family you are will affect your choice of childcare. If you value your privacy, for example, you may want to avoid the live-in option, whether au pair or nanny. If you like your home to be immaculate, if you work from there, or if you live in a small house or flat, you might prefer childcare outside the home – a childminder or nursery, a nannyshare at another house – so you can minimise wear and tear. If you value one-to-one care, you might prefer to employ a nanny who can give your child undivided attention in the security of his home environment. If you are an active, outdoor family you will be looking for lots of outdoor opportunities for play, and may prefer the flexibility of a nanny over the restricted options at a city nursery. Lots of factors will influence the decision you eventually make, and reading the sections and the chapters that follow will help you determine what types of care will fit best with your family. Thankfully, there are so many choices available these days that most families are likely to find an arrangement that suits them.

YOUR BASIC CHILDCARE OPTIONS

Just as every family is different, so are the needs of every child within that family. Just as families differ in their personal, financial and work circumstances, children differ in age, personality and development, and the childcare we choose needs to take all of that into account.

Here, I have summarised your basic childcare options, first in a list with a brief description, then set out in a table, which may help you to eliminate some straight away. For example, if you have a newborn baby you will not be able to use wraparound care or an au pair. I have not included playgroups where parents accompany their children as they are not generally considered to constitute childcare as such. Costs are expressed in general terms.

I have separated early-days childcare from the later stages. To begin with, if you need help at home with your baby or children, consider the following options – in general you will be around the house so the carer will not have 'sole charge' and the position is likely to be temporary.

When you go back to work, or if you are looking for ongoing help, you are likely to want to leave your children in the carer's sole charge. This means introducing the option of care outside the home as well as at home.

Temporary help at home in the early days

Maternity nurse – for newborns, usually live-in, either days or nights (but usually both) for a few days or few weeks

Doula – support through birth and/or the first few weeks with new baby from (usually) an experienced mother

Night nanny – night-time care for the first few weeks with a new baby

Mother's help – help with childcare and housework at any age or stage

Relatives and friends – for the lucky few!

Permanent help when you go back to work

Nanny – live-in or -out, at your home, part-time or full-time

Nannyshare – a nanny who works for two families so costs less

Workplace crèche – if you are lucky enough to have one

Day nursery or children's centre – part-/full-time centre-based care

Montessori nursery or sessional care – part-/full-time

Childminder – part-/full-time care in her own home

Before- and after-school, holiday clubs – school-based for children aged 5+

Au pair – live-in part-time help with school-age children (5+)

Wraparound care – school-based for 2–5s

Relatives and friends – on a commercial or non-commercial basis

The chart on pages 26–7 offers a guide to the main features of each type of childcare. The column headings list the main areas in which the types of childcare vary.

Live-in or -out Live-in means that the childcarer will sleep at your house, either on a temporary basis (night-nanny or temporary live-in nanny) or on a permanent or long-term basis (permanent live-in nanny or au pair).

Full-time or part-time Some parents need childcare either for part-days (after-school care, mother's help in the mornings only, au pair or babysitter) or for part of the week (Monday–Wednesday or every other Thursday, for example). Some types of childcarer are restricted in what they can offer in this respect (e.g. au pairs, night-nannies) but others are flexible (nannies, nurseries, relatives).

Hours Maternity nurses are unusual in that they are 'on call' technically 24 hours a day for new babies, but most childcare settings operate within set hours, and nannies rarely work more than a standard 11-hour day (12 hours for live-ins). If you work shifts or unusual hours, it can be harder to find childcare to suit your needs, and you may have to combine various forms to find the right solution.

Cost Costs will vary across the country and from year to year, but the table will give you an indication of whether the childcare setting is expensive, moderate or inexpensive. There is more detail on cost within each chapter and more on financing childcare in Appendix 2.

Registration/inspection The chapters that follow deal with registration and inspection in relation to each childcare setting. In a nutshell, the settings that require official registration and are inspected by Ofsted are nurseries and childminders. Nannies have the option of registering (and parents can benefit financially from that) but doulas and maternity nurses do not. The table overleaf indicates whether or not registration is possible and whether it is compulsory.

Year-round care While a day nursery is open all year, and usually only closed briefly at Christmas, other childcare settings operate in term-time only. Nannies and childminders, although they work year-round, will take holiday during the year, but this should not normally exceed the holiday you will be taking as an employee.

Ages of children Some childcarers (e.g. nannies, childminders) can work with children and babies of any age, and others (nursery schools, au pairs) are limited in the ages they care for. See the list on page 29 for specific advice on childcare for school-age children.

AT-A-GLANCE GUIDE TO CHILDCARE SUITABILITY

TYPE OF CHILDCARE	Live-in or -out	Full-time	Part-time	Hours	How expensive (see website for approximate current costs)	Registered or inspected?	Year-round care	Ages of children	Page
Maternity nurse	Either	Yes	Yes	24	Expensive	No	Yes	Babies	42
Doula	Out	Yes	Yes	Flexible	Expensive	No	Yes	Babies	47
Night nanny	In	No	Yes	6 p.m.–8 a.m.	Expensive	Registerable	Yes	Babies	51
Mother's help	Either	Yes	Yes	Flexible	Moderate	Registerable	Yes	All	55
Nanny	Either	Yes	Yes	Flexible	Expensive	Registerable	Yes	All	61
Nannyshare	Either	Yes	Yes	Flexible	Moderate	Registerable	Yes	All	123
Friends/ relatives	Out	Yes	Yes	Free	Free	No	Yes	All	249
Au pair/ au pair plus	In	No	Yes	Varies	Inexpensive	No	Yes	3+	145

Babysitter	Out	No	Yes	Evenings	Moderate	No	Yes	All	172
Childminder	Out	Yes	Yes	Varies	Inexpensive	Yes	Yes	All	181
Day nursery	n/a	Yes	Yes	7.30–6	Moderate	Yes	Yes	Under 5	203
Children's centre	n/a	Yes	Yes	7.30–6.30	Moderate	Yes	Yes	Under 5	221
Montessori nursery	n/a	Yes	Yes	Varies	Moderate	Yes	Varies	2–5	312
Nursery school and playgroups	n/a	Yes	Yes	a.m. or p.m.	Moderate	Yes	No	2–5	229
Workplace crèche	n/a	Yes	Yes	8–6	Moderate	Yes	Varies	Under 5	220
Before-/after-school club	n/a	No	Yes	8–9 3.30–6	Inexpensive	Yes	Yes	5+	240
Wraparound care	n/a	No	Yes	Varies	Inexpensive	Yes	Yes	2+	241

In the early stages it's important to look at the major differences between childcare in your home and out of your home. Here is a list of the advantages of each.

In the home

- Convenient – no need to take/collect
- Continuity – less settling in
- No 'other people's children'
- Flexible schedule and activities
- Flexible hours
- Child can still be cared for if sick
- Siblings can stay together
- Suitable for children of different ages

At work or outside the home

- Cheaper
- Sociable (especially for single children)
- Less wear and tear on the home
- No hidden costs (nanny's lunch, petrol, tax and NI)
- If nursery staff are ill, they are replaced
- Good for families in flats or smaller houses

AS YOUR CHILDREN GROW UP

When you have one small baby, whether you opt for nursery, nanny, childminder or even relatives, the choices are relatively straightforward, and without any other commitments during the day, there is flexibility in where your child can be cared for and by whom. When you have more children, however, and when they reach school age, the arrangements can become slightly more complicated. Many parents come to my agency looking for before- and after-school care, hoping to find a nanny willing to work for an hour in the morning and three or four hours in the afternoon. Not surprisingly, such candidates are hard to find, and usually limited to students with academic commitments during the school day. There are, however, a number of alternatives to embarking on a search for one of these elusive 'students', so don't despair at this point and give up work! Here are your main options if your children are at school.

- Nanny: possibly student as described above, who has studying commitments during school day; see Chapter 4, page 61.
- Nannyshare: she looks after a baby or other children during the school day, but bear in mind you will probably have that baby/children at your house after school and during the holidays; see Chapter 5, page 123.
- Nannyshare: the nanny brings her own baby to work with her; see Chapter 5, page 138.
- Au pair: if you have room in your house; see Chapter 6, page 145.
- Childminder: she looks after some children all day, and others before and after school; see Chapter 7, page 181.
- Before- and after-school clubs and holiday care (through the Extended Schools Scheme or privately); see Chapter 9, page 240.
- Relatives; see Chapter 10, page 249.

WHEN AND WHERE TO START LOOKING FOR CHILDCARE

Parents never cease to be amazed by how far in advance they are expected to organise care for their offspring. It is not uncommon for popular nurseries and childminders to be booked up so far ahead that you need to register your interest as soon as you see the little blue line in the pregnancy test kit. Here is a summary chart showing roughly how far ahead you should set up the different types of childcare available, and whom you should contact about each one.

Type	How far ahead	Where to ask (see resources section for details and useful websites)
Nursery	asap	Local authority, recommendations
Childminder	asap	Local authority, recommendations
Nanny	6–8 weeks ahead	Agency, recommendations, Internet, childcare publications
Au pair	6–8 weeks ahead	Agency, recommendations, Internet
School-based care	Any time	Local authority, school
Maternity nurse	asap	Agency, recommendations, Internet

SETTLING IN

Settling a child into a new scenario may take time, and is harder with a nursery or childminder than with a new nanny because the setting is unfamiliar. Toddlers may be harder to settle than babies as they may be clingy and more likely to resist being left. In the case of childcare outside the home, you may want to accompany your child on a first visit, then make another short one, popping out for a few minutes, leaving him with the childminder or nursery staff. Whatever setting you choose, when you hand him over in the mornings, it is best to do so decisively and leave promptly. It's not unusual for a child to be upset at first when he is left but, with time, this should change.

Selina has three children, all of whom went to nursery, and all of whom reacted differently:

I was very, very anxious leaving Toby, my eldest, but he seemed utterly unperturbed by being left. I was almost disappointed at how quickly he settled in. Molly, my second, was unsure at first, and did a bit of clinging and crying, but after a week she toddled in very willingly. Funnily enough, it was my youngest who put up the biggest fight. She would howl as soon as she saw the nursery and grip me very tightly. I think it would have broken my heart but the nursery staff, whom I knew very well by then, assured me that as soon as I was out of sight she completely cheered up. It never changed, and although I suffered a little bit every morning, I got used to it, and now when I tell her what a fuss she made she laughs and tells me she loved it really . . .

YOUR CHILDCARE PLAN

You've heard of birth plans, you've heard of business plans: this is a childcare plan. If you take into account from the outset all of the different criteria that will influence your childcare choice, you are more likely to make the right decision.

Your plan will involve the following decisions:

- whether to go back to work
- when to go back to work
- how to go back to work – full- or part-time, possibly on a flexible basis

You will also need to know, and the chapters that follow will show you:

- how easy it will be to get childcare to fit your working time. Sometimes supply and demand may mean you have to buy more childcare than you need – read about the availability of different types of carer in the following chapters to assess how likely you are to have to do that
- how much that childcare will cost, whether any cost savings (vouchers, tax credits) apply. Look at the cost section of each type of provision and what incentives are available

You will need to take into account all your responsibilities and all the demands on your time when you work out how much childcare you need. Think about producing a pie chart like the one below which shows how you might spend your average working day. It should help you to focus on the extent of your non-work responsibilities, and how they might need sharing out or delegating if you are going to hold down a job as well:

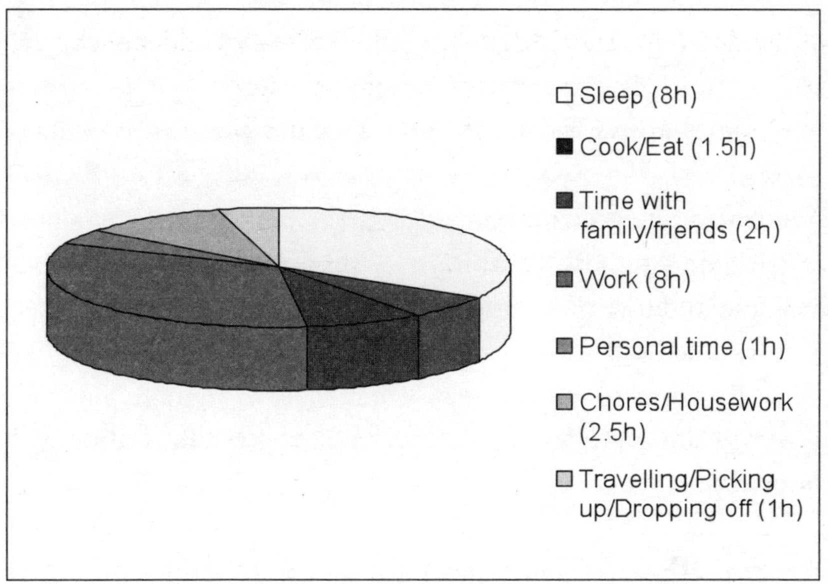

Don't forget to think about how much time you spend:

- going through the post, filing, household administration
- dealing with children's social life and extra-curricular activities
- talking to and just 'being with' your children
- helping children with homework and reading
- picking up and dropping off children

Using the information you gather, start to draw up your childcare plan. The format overleaf is a good starting point and will focus your mind on issues you may not have considered bringing into the picture. You may be able to fill in the sections straight away, but make sure you discuss them with your partner or you may find yourself starting from scratch when he points out that he can't come home at lunchtime on a Friday . . .

EXAMPLE CHILDCARE PLAN

My vision of how we are going to live and work as a family is [describe here how you see things – who is going to work when and where, what sort of hours, same job/new job – include how much time you will spend individually and together with your children and give an overall picture of your life together]

As well as time for work, we need childcare to cover [nights out, going to the gym, domestic responsibilities] **totalling about** [ ] **hours per** [day/week]

My major priority is [keeping career going/taking a full year maternity leave/making time for leisure activities]

[Partner's] **major priority is** [being a devoted husband and father/earning enough money to support the family/playing golf on a Friday]

The childcare will start from [think here whether you will need childcare before you go back to work: mothers' helps and maternity nurses (see pages 55 and 42) can do a lot to keep you sane in the early weeks with a new baby especially after your partner has returned to work]

This is how we will divide house-related chores [shopping, cooking, admin, gardening]

One thing I don't want to compromise on is

One thing [partner] **doesn't want to compromise on is**

The kind of childcare we need is [either complete what you think you need or leave blank until you have read further]

- [type of childcare]
- [ ] days per week
- [ ] hours per day
- [expected cost]
- [to be reviewed after . . .]

> ***Louise*** *had always assumed she and her husband, Martin, would share the childcare outside their full-time jobs in HR and marketing. After the birth of their first baby, Louise took six months off, then went back four days a week. On those four days she and Martin would take it in turns to pick up Emma from nursery in the evenings. What she hadn't planned for was Martin working extra-long hours on Friday when she stayed at home, apparently assuming that all the household chores would have been done by the weekend. 'I thought we wanted to spend weekends doing things together as a family,' he said to her, most put out that she could complain about his expectations of her. 'But I'm working four days so I can spend time with Emma, not dash around doing chores all day.'*

It makes life easier if you imagine such scenarios before they hit you and agree on how you will share tasks.

WHAT'S IN THE WAY?

It may sound straightforward enough but the reality of handing over your children to another person can bring with it a lot of negative feelings. Men tend to be generally immune from pressure to stay at home and be a full-time parent, but women get it from all angles. If you are racked by guilt and can't see the wood for the trees because of it, if you feel unworthy of going back to work, or if you think it doesn't make financial sense, listen to the voice in your head (you may find complete fulfilment as an at-home parent) but read the next sections before you go along with it.

SOCIAL PRESSURE

The problem You will see another mum happily pushing a buggy down the road with a gaggle of friends, then again at lunchtime, enjoying a glass of wine outside a café, spooning purée into the baby's mouth, laughing as if this is the pinnacle of her happiness.

The solution You'll meet these deliriously happy women everywhere, but there are a few things to remember before you jump on their bandwagon.

- They may work on all the other days of the week.
- They may have been up all night but are putting on a brave face because they feel they need to be seen to be happy.
- They may be the nanny.
- One day that child will be at school six hours a day and his mother may find it hard to get a job.

GUILT

The problem Believe it or not, stay-at-home mothers suffer from as much stereotyping and criticism in the press and society as working mothers, but it is the mothers who go back to work who tend to feel more guilt about their decision. Don't ignore outright any feelings of guilt about leaving your children in childcare. Questions may need to be answered before those concerns can be dealt with and put to rest. All mothers want their children to grow up happy, healthy and successful, and most of us wonder (and often worry about) how our personal choices will affect our children's futures. We are constantly bombarded with reports telling us what is 'best' for our children, from cutting out E numbers, to naps in the afternoon, to omega 3, but it is on childcare that the statistics appear to be in a constant state of flux. Nurseries have been alternately slated and eulogised by conflicting research, only adding to public confusion.

A common reaction to the media pressure is to feel pervasive and non-specific guilt about whatever choices we make. It is somehow more acceptable to feel guilty than it is to laugh about or feel angry at the ridiculous expectations placed upon us. But why are women so susceptible to being judged? Author Stephanie Calman's view is that we are not setting our own goals but allowing others to set them for us, then 'failing'. She says: 'If you want to open the floodgates to serious guilt, just use childcare. Having your mother mind your kids is fine, even if she's a borderline psychopath who drinks sherry while they wander into the road. Paying someone is different. The newspapers love to cite research that shows nurseries make children aggressive, or turn them into shoplifters, or are the root of all society's ills. When I read that stuff – with the evidence to the contrary playing happily beside me – I feel bad about it all over again. It's as if the guilt is never expiated but merely dormant, able to be reactivated at any time.'

The solution Rather than worrying about the views of the in-laws, or mothers at the school gate, make decisions about the factors you do control, and talk to older children to find out how what you do influences them. Ultimately, if something is right for you then at some level it will probably be right for your family too. Jessica sees it quite simply:

> *When I've had a good day at work, my children definitely share the benefit of that with me. I am physically and mentally recharged, much more attentive and enthusiastic, and enjoy my time with them more. They bring me stories of what they've been doing at school and nursery, and I bring my renewed energy to their lives.*

CHILDCARE COSTS

The problem Nannies are just too expensive

The solution There are less expensive options than a top-flight nanny – a childminder can cost you as little as £30 per day, and a place in a Sure Start children's centre even less than that. Begin by deducting the cost from your joint salaries, not just your own salary: don't assume that you should stay at home unless it is financially worthwhile according to your sole earning power. If the children have a working father, then he can shoulder a proportion of the cost. Your salary is also likely to increase as you progress up the career ladder. Most employers nowadays offer a salary-sacrifice scheme to help their employees pay for registered childcare, and it is also worth noting that there are free childcare places on offer for three- to four-year-olds at all nurseries. Tax credits are available to parents on low incomes but, remarkably, only one in three parents takes advantage of the help available.

SELF-ESTEEM

The problem There's nothing like pregnancy, childbirth and looking after a baby all day for getting to your sense of self-worth. Without the affirmation of the workplace and other adults, and with sleepless nights, and days spent constantly on call for no obvious reward, we may take a dip psychologically and emotionally. The celebrity back-in-your-jeans-in-two-weeks culture doesn't help. These days, post-natal depression is less of a taboo subject, but there are many levels at which mothers find it hard to cope and feel inadequate, which can increase to a general sense of unworthiness when the very notion of stepping back on to the trading floor or into the boardroom may seem impossible.

The solution Men: if your partner is at home alone with a newborn day in day out, she needs a medal every day, or at least a bunch of flowers every week. (Oh, and don't forget to change the water and then throw them away when they die.) Mothers need to feel genuinely appreciated to have a chance of firing on all cylinders. And to all mothers out there, yes, you have a new role, but you are the same capable, lovable, respected person you were before you had your baby. Think of it as an identity *in addition to*, rather than *replacing*, your old one. Motherhood will teach you patience, perseverance, diplomacy, multi-tasking and budget-management; you will become a nurturer, a listener, a negotiator and an achiever. With all these new and finely honed skills, how can you think of depriving the workplace of your valuable presence? They need you now more than ever. The Resources section, pages 313–32, includes information on recruitment websites specifically directed at mothers looking for employment.

SUMMARY

Have you considered:

- whether, when and how to go back to work?
- what forms of childcare you are interested in generally?
- the cost implications of returning to work?
- when you need to start looking for childcare?
- how you will delegate and share responsibilities with your partner and within the childcare scenario?

Whether you are working or not, and whether or not you have even reached a decision about returning to work, you may still like to go on to learn more about what childcare options are available to you now. Chapter 3 deals with getting help in the early days when you will be at your most exhausted. Once you feel you have addressed the primary considerations of whether, when and how to go back to work, you will be ready to move on to the subsequent chapters which deal with nannies, nurseries, childminders, etc.

CHAPTER 3

Maternity Nurses, Doulas, Night Nannies and Mothers' Helps

When your new baby arrives, your world will turn upside down. No antenatal class or pregnancy manual quite prepares you for the exhaustion you will experience after weeks of sleepless nights, or for the sheer amount of time a newborn takes up. Capable, high-achieving mums are stunned by the fact that they cannot fit simple routine tasks into their day any more: 'Now I think it's a real result if I just clear away the breakfast things,' one new mum confesses. 'Just accept that nothing is going to get done,' says another, 'or you'll end up depressed.'

Mothers are harsh judges of themselves, and will set themselves unfeasibly high standards in the most difficult circumstances. Media pressure, from celebrity mothers getting back to size zero within days to advice columns on how soon you should get back to the office after giving birth, may make the average new mother feel inadequate, unattractive and an inevitable disappointment to her partner.

Hence the very welcome help in the home. Without a team of maiden aunts and sprightly grannies champing at the bit to get their hands on our new infant, we are these days more likely to have to pay for the help we need, and thankfully, there is an army of qualified, experienced childcarers out there ready to step in and work alongside new mothers to make the most of those first precious weeks. This chapter shows what help is available to new parents at home, starting with the early days when sleep is like gold dust . . .

MATERNITY NURSES

The maternity nurse is one of the most valuable (and unfortunately the most costly) resources in the childcare market, to which the supply/demand ratio testifies. You will usually need to book one several months ahead of your due date.

On duty 24 hours a day, six days a week, her role is primarily to help you with all aspects of caring for your newborn, from breastfeeding and bathing to establishing a good baby routine and, most importantly, helping you to get back on your feet.

An experienced maternity nurse will often have her tried and tested ways of working with a family, and a new mother will usually be grateful for her confidence and ability to take control.

A maternity nurse may be a good option for you if:

- this is your first baby and you feel there's a lot to learn
- you have more than one child and need your sleep so that you can cope with the other(s)

- you have more than one baby and have other arrangements in place for the care of siblings
- you want someone to concentrate exclusively on you and the baby rather than help generally
- you have had a difficult birth or twins, or a previous difficult experience with a new baby, and want to make sure you get it right
- you are a lone parent and need an extra pair of hands to help you cope
- you are happy with someone living in (although live-out maternity nurses are available)
- cost is not an issue

DUTIES

The maternity nurse will usually be experienced and able to tell you exactly what duties she will perform in your home. They will include:

- primarily baby-centred care, but she will offer you moral support and teach you how to be comfortable with your baby
- night feeds: she will usually sleep with the baby and either bring her to you for a feed, or will bottle-feed
- advice on breastfeeding, bathing and establishing a routine
- dealing with the baby's laundry, sterilising bottles, making up formula feeds

She will not look after other siblings or take responsibility for school runs, etc., unless this has been agreed beforehand.

QUALIFICATIONS

Most maternity nurses are nannies with specific maternity qualifications and considerable experience of newborns, but some are registered nurses, midwives, neo-natal nurses or health visitors. There are a number of courses for maternity nurses, the most popular of which is the Maternity Practitioner Award. Agencies usually require maternity nurses to have some childcare qualification and at least two years' post-qualification experience with babies under one.

COST

Live-in maternity nurses cost £120–40 per 24-hour period. They usually take care of their own tax and National Insurance contributions because they are self-employed. However, since you will book a maternity nurse well in advance of the birth it may happen that your baby hasn't arrived by the time she is due to start work. You should make sure that you know what payment she expects for any period of waiting, but be prepared to pay her half of her rate for the first week and possibly the full amount for the second. If you have private health cover and have had a Caesarean or birth complications, you may find you can reclaim the cost of a maternity nurse.

HOURS

A maternity nurse usually lives in and is usually on call 24 hours a day, six days a week. However, these days there are plenty of live-out maternity nurses who prefer to work more conventional hours.

PROS

- You will have more sleep than you would otherwise get because the maternity nurse will do the night feeds.
- She will provide you with essential all-round support during those physically and mentally exhausting first few weeks after childbirth.
- She will provide particularly valuable support if you have had a Caesarean or twins.

CONS

- A maternity nurse is expensive.
- If you are not used to having other people in the house her presence may seem intrusive.
- You may feel out of control or helpless if someone else takes over to such an extent.
- You won't learn by trial and error if everything is done for you at this stage in the baby's life.

WHERE TO FIND A MATERNITY NURSE

Most maternity nurses are registered with agencies. Although it is advisable to book one several months before your due date, it is always worth ringing round the agencies if you decide you would like one at the last minute – an emergency maternity nurse may be available. Some agencies specialise in maternity nurses but most nanny agencies have them on their books. In all cases you should take up at least two written references on the phone.

Emma says:

I had a maternity nurse to help me get through the first few weeks with my daughter. My son Freddy was one at the time and a real handful, so it made sense to spend the money on getting the new baby into a routine so that I had a fighting chance of coping with two so close in age. Freddy was never a good sleeper and was going through a particularly demanding phase, and Jo, our maternity nurse, was keen to make sure that his needs were met as well as mine and the baby's. One night, when I was attempting to get some much-needed sleep in the spare room, Freddy simply refused to settle in his cot. He took Jo and my husband by the hand, led them to our room and made clear he wanted the two of them to get into bed together so he could sleep between them. Fortunately we all had a good enough sense of humour to overcome the embarrassment of the situation, and my husband was far too tired to think about anything except sleep . . .

INTERVIEWING A MATERNITY NURSE

With the arrival of a new baby, the last thing you need is the added stress of managing a difficult relationship with a stranger in your home. When you interview your maternity nurse, concentrate on how comfortable you feel with her: you will be living in close proximity to her for several weeks. Here are some general guidelines for interview questions.

- Discuss the details of her qualifications and experience.
- What are her views on bottle- versus breastfeeding? It is

important that she supports you in the decision you make.

- What are her views on routines? Does she go with the flow of demand feeding or encourage routine from the outset? A really good maternity nurse should say that she likes to meet a baby before deciding on any specific routine.
- What are her views on the way in which you will work together? For example, will she object to you visiting your baby in the middle of the night?
- Discuss any proposed use of baby monitors.
- Discuss her experience of medical or feeding problems, including colic and reflux.
- Discuss your family time and her time off. She will need a day off each week and you will need time alone with your baby.

DOULAS

'*Doula*' (pronounced 'doola') is a Greek word meaning 'woman servant or caregiver' but it is used today to refer to an experienced woman (often a mother herself) who offers emotional and practical support to another woman (or a couple) before, during and after childbirth. She functions as a member of the extended family would in 'mothering the mother'. Her task is to ensure that you are empowered and fulfilled during pregnancy, birth and the early days as a new mother. This type of support also helps the whole family to relax and enjoy the experience. A doula will live out, and will usually work a few hours each day in your home.

A doula might be the right childcare option for you if:

- you like the idea of a holistic approach
- you like the idea of support from another mother with experience of her own babies
- you have a busy household and need general help
- you want live-out help around the time of your baby's birth, not live-in
- you are looking for support before as well as during and after the birth
- you have other children who need looking after
- childcare qualifications aren't your main priority

DUTIES

Like a maternity nurse, a doula will have a good idea of her remit, but here is a basic list of what you can expect.

- Help and support for you and your family before, during and after the birth of the baby.
- Support and advice during labour, alongside a midwife but without a medical role.
- Breastfeeding support and advice.
- Care of older children.
- Family shopping and meals.
- General household chores including laundry.

QUALIFICATIONS

Many doulas don't have formal qualifications but have had children themselves so understand the traumas of childbirth and the crucial first few weeks. However, there are now accredited doula training courses running all over the UK, which add value to the real-life experience element so that doulas can provide valuable emotional support during labour and really professional post-natal care.

COST

Doulas charge £10–15 per hour, highest rates usually being charged in London and the south east. You can hire a 'birth doula' who will charge between £200 and £500. The fees vary from individual to individual.

HOURS

Doulas usually work a minimum of four hours per day. You can hire a doula for a week or two, or several months, depending on your needs.

PROS

- Support and advice without the level of intervention offered by a maternity nurse.
- Will take on general duties, which a night nanny or maternity nurse will not.

CONS

- Cost – higher than a mother's help, for example.
- You may find it difficult to hand over your entire role as

mother and 'manager of domestic operations', as one mother put it – some feel a sense of helplessness with a doula in the house.

- No qualifications required.

WHERE TO FIND A DOULA

Try nanny agencies and specific doula agencies. Google is a good start.

Vanessa says:

I first used a doula 10 years ago with the birth of my first baby, Zoe. I had no idea what to expect but someone put me in touch with a local lady she had used and found to be brilliant. I didn't bother checking any more references as she came from a trusted source, but we met and chatted for a couple of hours before I decided to go ahead. With a husband working long hours and no family living close by, I needed all the help I could get. I was also very nervous about the whole thing, and really appreciated having someone who had been through it several times and could keep me calm and reassured.

Grace started helping me a few hours a day before the birth, getting everything ready in the baby's room, helping me choose things like sterilisers and nappies, and she was waiting at the house when we got home with the baby, and came in every day for three weeks after that, again just for a few hours a day. It was like having a lovely granny to dote on us all. She cooked my meals, looked after the baby so I could catch up on sleep and gave me that extra confidence in my abilities as a mother. Grace came back to us when our next baby was born, but by the time we had our third we had moved away. I didn't feel like taking on anyone else because I didn't think anyone could fill her shoes, but she taught me so much and inspired me so much that I almost didn't need the help the third time round.

INTERVIEWING A DOULA

When interviewing a doula you should ask many of the same questions you would put to a maternity nurse. However, rather than teaching, as a maternity nurse does, she will help. Make sure you agree on the main aspects of childcare and family routines, and that her attitudes to punctuality, tidiness, food and nutrition are similar to yours. Also, she needs to get on not only with you but with your other child(ren) if she is to work with them. Find out as much as you can about her own experience of having and bringing up children – this may help you decide if she is the right person for you.

NIGHT NANNIES

Night nannies are daily nannies on the night shift, primarily concerned with getting a baby through the night with a view to establishing a good sleep routine while you get some rest and your sanity back. They are less likely than maternity nurses or doulas to train you in breastfeeding. Many hire a night nanny when things get too much for them, so you don't necessarily need to book too far ahead.

A night nanny might be the right childcare option for you if:

- you don't mind someone spending nights in your house
- you want someone qualified and experienced
- getting sleep is a priority for you
- you and your partner are away from home and your daytime childcare is not available for the night shift
- cost is not an issue

DUTIES

The night nanny's main duties are:

- to feed, change and settle the baby during the night
- to sterilise bottles and make up formula as necessary
- to dress the baby in the morning
- to help and advise on sleep routines
- to allow you a lie-in

She is not responsible for domestic cleaning or laundry.

QUALIFICATIONS

A night nanny need not be qualified (there is no legal requirement for any nanny to have a qualification), but you should *expect* her to have a qualification in childcare (see Appendix 5), and to have particular and significant experience of newborns.

COST

The cost of a night nanny varies greatly from area to area but is generally about 10 per cent above the local hourly net rate charged by daily nannies.

HOURS

Night nannies usually work between 9 p.m. and 7 a.m., and agencies recommend they work for you on one to three nights per week. You can have one every night, of course, but the cost will mount up, and you may feel a bit left out. A placement may last from a couple of nights to several months. If you are using an agency, and only taking a night nanny for a couple of nights a week, be aware that you may be sent a different one each time.

PROS

- A night nanny is easy to book and 'install' in your home, as she doesn't need to get to grips with the whole house, just the baby, nappies and formula.
- You get more sleep.

CONS

- If you are breastfeeding during the day, you may experience a drop in milk level if a nanny is feeding the baby during the night.
- The cost – you are spending money in your sleep.
- The nanny is usually temporary so doesn't become part of the family.

WHERE TO FIND A NIGHT NANNY

Most nanny agencies supply night nannies, and some specialise in this area.

Jo writes:

We had a night nanny for a week when Hugo was three weeks old and I was absolutely exhausted. My husband had gone back to work and wasn't helping so much any more, and I wasn't coping very well on my own. I chose a night nanny because I was desperate for the sleep, and would pay any money to get it, but didn't want too much intrusion in the house. I felt confident that if I slept properly I wouldn't have a problem getting the baby into a routine in the daytime. I felt slightly uncomfortable with the idea of someone being in the house 'teaching' me how to be a proper mother. Hadn't women done this for centuries? Of course, it wasn't as simple as that. The nanny was fabulous, we hardly saw her, and I had plenty of sleep at night. However, she was doing the night feeds with a bottle, and I couldn't express fast enough to keep up. My milk supply dwindled and we had the baby on formula before I would have chosen to. However, I know other mothers who didn't have this problem. I think you have to work out your priorities, and mine was sleep! I would definitely do the same again.

INTERVIEWING A NIGHT NANNY

You will be looking for someone with experience and qualifications similar to those of a maternity nurse, and will be asking similar questions about demand-feeding and routines. It will be less important for you to establish a bond with your night nanny, as you will see so little of her, so you are likely to focus more on proven technical ability and following up references (see page 95, Checking References).

MOTHERS' HELPS

As the job title suggests, a mother's help primarily assists a mother, working alongside her in all aspects of her daily routine. She may live in or out, but today is more likely to live out. Live-in mothers' helps are generally supplied by au-pair agencies and will come from overseas, working slightly longer hours than an au pair. (See Chapter 6, page 162.) A mother's help usually has relatively little childcare experience, or is using the position as a stepping-stone, moving from nursery work to nannying. Although mothers' helps are not trained to work unsupervised, you will probably want to leave her with your children at some point, and will expect her to gain confidence on the job to take sole responsibility. Essentially, a mother's help is an extra pair of (safe) hands around the house.

A mother's help might be the childcare solution for you if:

- you are going to be at home most of the time
- you want flexible, general help rather than just childcare
- qualifications aren't important to you
- native English is not important
- you are happy with live-out help (although some do live in)
- you like having company

DUTIES

A mother's help's duties should be set out in a written contract, and you can find a template for this in Appendix 1 (pages 283–91), but here is a basic list of what you can expect.

- Help with looking after the children.
- Help with household chores including laundry and ironing.
- Help with shopping and planning and preparing meals.

QUALIFICATIONS

No qualifications are required of a mother's help – although, ironically, she may typically have a Slovakian business degree. If you are going to leave your mother's help with sole charge of your baby or children, consider asking her to do a first-aid course or, even better, a basic childcare course. See pages 327–8 for suggestions.

COST

A mother's help will cost you slightly less than a nanny on an hourly basis, but as the definitions are blurred, so is the salary difference. Also, while it is relatively easy to fill a sole-charge nanny position, it can be a challenge to find a mother's help with decent English who is happy to take on a shared-charge role – reflected in what you end up paying her.

HOURS

The hours a mother's help works will vary, and it is up to you to come to an agreement with her. If you are trying to make the job appealing and bring in the maximum number of candidates, bear in mind that unless they have studying commitments, they generally like to work full rather than part days (10–11 hours). If you do need someone for part days, mornings are easier than afternoons because of the huge demand for after-school carers.

PROS

- Flexible job description.
- Not strictly childcare – more like cloning yourself.
- Can be good company.

CONS

- Unqualified and unregulated.
- Job doesn't appeal to experienced childcarers so calibre of candidates is lower.
- Candidates are young and inexperienced so require training – including language!

Martine, a full-time mother of three, finds her mother's help a godsend:

> *My mother's help has been brilliant. Not only has she given me the freedom to start a little business at home, but I can spend more time with the kids as she doesn't mind doing the Sainsbury's run and hoovering for me while I take them to the park. I was worried that if I had a nanny she wouldn't want to do those things and she would be spending time with the kids while I did the shopping, but with a mother's help you get the flexibility you need – it's sort of like having a wife . . .*

WHERE TO FIND A MOTHER'S HELP

Most nanny agencies will supply mothers' helps, or you can try advertising locally or online (see Resources, page 323). Since you are likely to pay an introduction fee to an agency for a candidate with relatively little childcare experience, it makes sense to go the DIY route first: use your networks to find recommendations, but make sure you do your homework and check all references thoroughly before you let anyone start work.

Here is Linda's story.

I found my mother's help through a local agency. She worked part-time for me and part-time for a neighbour so we shared the agency fee. Veronika was from Slovakia, had fluent English, a degree in economics, and was the eldest of five sisters. She was amazing from the word go, and my friend and I resolved to do everything possible to keep her as long as we could. My situation is difficult as I have a disability, which limits what I can do in terms of lifting my children, and on the days I don't work I need help all day from someone who has to follow me around doing what I can't do. Veronika did exactly that, and stayed with me until my youngest went to nursery, at which point my needs diminished. The other three days she worked for the other family in more of a nanny capacity, with lots of sole charge, and although she wasn't qualified she proved more than capable. Intelligence and common sense count for an awful lot when you're dealing with children and housework.

INTERVIEWING A MOTHER'S HELP

This is a tricky task. You want her to be your mirror image, with the same attitude, skills, standards and expertise, yet you are probably sitting across the sofa from a 19-year-old Macedonian with a dubious command of English and whose experience amounts to babysitting her six-year-old cousin last summer. Chances are that she has never lived independently and has never even contemplated juggling the housework, cooking and babycare as you have been doing for months. So, first, don't expect miracles. Look for initiative, energy, common sense and a pleasant personality you could work alongside, as well as a personality that is going to work for your children as well. Take up references on the phone, if for no other reason than to check for a history of dishonesty.

SUMMARY

Have you considered:

- whether you need help in the early days after the baby arrives? (Consider all childcare covered in this chapter.)
- whether you would like that help to begin before the baby arrives? (Consider a doula/mother's help.)
- whether you want someone living in your house? (Consider a maternity nurse.)
- whether you are happy for someone to be spending nights at your house? (Consider a night nanny or maternity nurse.)
- whether you need help for more than just yourself and the baby? (Consider a mother's help or doula.)

- whether you would be more comfortable with the help of someone older who is a mother herself ? (Consider a doula.)
- whether you will need ongoing help beyond the first few months? (Consider a mother's help.)

CHAPTER 4

Nannies

WHAT IS A NANNY?

A nanny is a childcarer who may or may not have childcare qualifications and who looks after your child or children in your own home. She may live in or out, and may work with the child(ren) on her own (sole charge) or alongside a parent (shared charge).

THE DIFFERENCES BETWEEN A NANNY AND A MOTHER'S HELP

There is a fine line to be drawn between a shared-charge nanny and a mother's help, but parents and candidates usually have a good idea of which side of it they stand. The main differences are:

- ➤ You should feel confident to leave a nanny in sole charge of your children, even if the position is mostly shared charge.

- A nanny's main priority is childcare; a mother's help fulfils general duties. Employers often question whether a nanny will empty the dishwasher and collect the dry-cleaning, but these concerns can be resolved at interview, by managing expectations and with a carefully drafted contract.
- A nanny is likely to expect a slightly higher hourly rate than a mother's help.
- Even if a nanny isn't qualified, she should have experience of caring for children of a similar age to your own.
- A mother's help may be a complete beginner.

THE DIFFERENCES BETWEEN A NANNY AND A CHILDMINDER

- A childminder works in her own home; a nanny works in the home of the child(ren) she is caring for.
- A childminder must be registered; although a registration system exists for nannies, it is not compulsory.
- A nanny is more expensive than a childminder.
- You have more control over a nanny's duties and what your children do during the day.
- A nanny will look after your children only (and those of a family you choose to share her with). A childminder looks after children from several different families at once, and you will have no say in who they are.

THE DIFFERENCES BETWEEN A NANNY AND A NURSERY

- Cost: if you have one child, it may seem hard to justify the cost of a nanny when a nursery comes in at around half the price.
- Sickness: if your child is ill, a nursery will not want her to infect the other children at the nursery, and will have a policy stating how long she must be kept at home. A child must usually remain at home for the first 48 hours of any course of antibiotics. During the early months of a baby's life, you may need to take quite a lot of time off work, or spend a substantial sum on emergency childcare (see page 66). Most agencies will charge a fee for a temporary placement, and most temporary nannies charge a higher rate than permanent ones.
- Peace of mind: most new parents feel instinctively more relaxed about the idea of their baby staying at home than sending her to nursery when she's a few months old. The guilt you may feel at going back to work may be assuaged to some degree by the thought of Mary Poppins giving her full attention to your new arrival . . .

TYPES OF NANNY

DAILY (LIVE-OUT) NANNY

A daily or live-out nanny comes to your house each weekday at hours agreed between you, say, 7.45 a.m. to 6.30 p.m. This option is great if you value your privacy and need some distance between your family and your childcarer, and you can avoid the friction that may result from a stranger living in your house. Most live-out nannies can manage an early start if they drive and/or live locally, and probably benefit from spending time away from their charges. Live-out nannies can be either full- or part-time – working full days for a full week, part days, or full days for part of the week.

LIVE-IN NANNY

As the name suggests, a live-in nanny occupies your house with you, having either the spare room or, in some cases, separate accommodation within your home, and works a slightly longer day than a live-out nanny, usually including some babysitting. They are usually full-time, but some families' live-in nannies work part of the week for them and the rest for another family. They are increasingly hard to find as more and more girls prefer to live separately from their employer. If you are struggling to find a live-in nanny, you might consider either a live-out nanny, or a combination of a live-out nanny and an au pair (see Chapter 6, pages 145–72).

NANNYSHARE

In this scenario, a nanny looks after your children and another family's at your home or theirs, or brings her own child to your home, thereby saving you money and providing your child with playmates. In some situations she may live in one family's home and work for them and another family. A nanny in a nannyshare may work full-time for both families, or part-time for both families (part days or part of the week) or a combination of the two, and her salary will be calculated accordingly. She will receive an increased rate (usually around 10 per cent) for the hours she works for both families simultaneously. (See also Chapter 5, page 123.)

AGES COVERED

A nanny can look after children of any age, but you should bear in mind her qualifications, experience and the needs of your children. Some qualifications cover all ages, such as the CACHE diploma; others – maternity-nurse courses, for example – focus only on babies. Some nannies love looking after babies but are less suited to older children, and vice versa. In my experience, they are honest about this, and referees will often tell you that a nanny was 'great with the baby, but not so good with the older ones'. If you have more than one child, you should take particular care to check with referees whether the nanny was equally committed to children of different ages within the family. It often happens that a nanny will dote on a newborn baby, make up delicious organic purées and push a buggy endlessly round the park, but is less adept at helping with homework, making junk models and playing football in the garden. It has been suggested that older children benefit from having a male nanny: see page 67.

TEMPORARY AND PERMANENT NANNIES

You may be looking for a long-term nanny to see your baby through from birth to becoming a big brother or sister to several siblings, or you may need temporary cover for a short, fixed period, usually if your normal arrangements fall through – for example, if your child is excluded from nursery through illness, or if your nanny is sick.

It can be harder to find a temporary nanny than a permanent one, mainly because most of us need permanent work to pay the bills. And you may be tempted to ask, 'Why is she not working?' when an agency sends you a list of nannies available to start tomorrow. The fact is, many nannies end up with a period of days or weeks between jobs, and rely on temporary work to fill the gaps. It's slightly harder to find a temp for a few months rather than a few days or weeks, but plenty of girls with travel plans or university courses that start later in the year may be looking to fill the months between.

Temps may charge a higher hourly rate than permanent nannies. This relates partly to supply and demand, but also to their being ready to hit the ground running with little induction or handover. If you employ a temp, don't cut any corners when it comes to checking credentials and references, however much of a rush you may be in, and follow all the procedures suggested on pages 95–101 as far as is reasonably possible.

EMERGENCY CHILDCARE

What happens when your nanny/au pair/childminder is ill or on holiday and you cannot rely on friends and family as back-up? In the USA most employers offer back-up childcare in some form, and this is becoming an increasingly common employee benefit in the UK as well: www.emergencychildcare.co.uk allows you to book back-up childcare using local nannies, nurseries or childminders. They have an increasing number of corporate subscriptions to the service: it gives employers peace of mind because their workers will not be absent through breakdown of childcare arrangements. If you are going back to work, find out whether your employer has any childcare back-up scheme in place. If not, consider suggesting it!

MALE OR FEMALE NANNY?

There has been a lot in the press over recent years about the advent of the 'manny' – the male nanny – but the publicity has been unmatched as yet by actuality: most UK agencies are unlikely to put forward male candidates, even if you specifically tell them you are open to the idea, because of the overall lack of supply, and a general trend for male nannies to prefer working with toddlers upwards.

Annie Merrylees, a former London nanny, co-founded My Big Buddy in 2006 with the specific purpose of specialising in the recruitment of male nannies. While she was working as a nanny, first for a single mother and then for a family where the father's work kept him constantly absent, she became acutely aware of the missing male element in children's lives: 'These children live with their mothers, hardly see their fathers, their teachers are all female and then to cap it all along comes a female nanny as well. This imbalance is and always has been very common, but the balance can be restored by introducing a positive male influence into the mix.' My Big Buddy, a 'manny' agency, is experiencing an increasing demand for mannies as mothers realise the value of this alternative to the traditional female childcarer. One happy client said that, since the arrival of their manny, her shy, retiring little boy had been transformed into the most forthcoming child in his class.

Tinies Childcare reports that they place about 30 male childcarers a year as both nannies and nursery nurses. Amanda Coxen at Tinies is enthusiastic about the male influence on children, particularly in a nursery staffed mainly by women, in a household where children are mostly boys or if the parents are a female couple: 'I think male childcarers can provide a stabilising and balancing effect in a predominantly female environment.' But the number of male nannies is consistently lower than the number of females on the market. It seems that, true to stereotype, it's mainly girls who like looking after children.

A male nanny might be a good solution for you if:

- you have a boy or boys in your family (although plenty of girls are cared for by mannies)
- your children are aged over two
- you are looking for cover for the never-ending school holidays
- your children live in a female-dominated household
- the children don't see enough of their father

The only reported downside of a male nanny won't come to you as much of a surprise – apparently their domestic skills may leave a lot to be desired . . .

IS A NANNY THE RIGHT OPTION FOR YOU?

A nanny (male or female) may be the right childcare choice if:

- you want a childcarer to fit in with your routine and lifestyle
- you want input into your child's routine, activities, meals, etc.
- you have children of different ages and want them to be cared for in the same setting by the same person
- you have a school-age child but work all day and would like him/her to be able to come home after school
- you have an extra bedroom (for a live-in nanny)
- you can afford it: remember, as an employee she will expect you to pay her tax and National Insurance contributions on top of her salary (see 'Cost' – page 71)

MYTHS AND REALITY

A sizeable proportion of the population still thinks of a nanny in the context of a Victorian nursery run by a stern, aproned woman in a cap who addresses you formally and presents your offspring to you for debriefing at bedtime. Others will picture a uniformed Norland nanny, working for the super-rich, with the same highly disciplined manner and zero tolerance of misbehaviour.

The reality is far from either stereotype. Nannies are no longer the privilege of the wealthy, and many work in ordinary homes. If both parents work, if there are school-age children and no other suitable or affordable options available locally, the family may have no choice but to employ a nanny. Although some Norland nannies still wear uniform, the decision is up to them and most choose not to. Similarly, it is rare for nannies to call their employers by anything other than their first names. Over recent years the huge influx of Eastern and Central European nannies has done much to dispel the myths. In London it might be a fair estimate that more than half of nannies currently employed are non-native-English speakers. Elsewhere in the UK there are fewer foreign nationals, but a higher concentration in the major cities.

DUTIES

A nanny's responsibilities can be many and varied, but you should be able to assume that she will:

- ensure the safety and well-being of the children in her care
- give the children affection, support and encouragement
- offer educational and creative stimulation
- organise and supervise social activities
- deal with correspondence from school/nursery
- provide nutritious meals
- shop for children's food/clothes if required
- bath the children
- keep a diary of activities showing developmental milestones
- keep bedrooms, kitchen and communal areas clean and tidy
- do the children's laundry
- take the children to the doctor, dentist and other medical appointments

This list is not exhaustive and you may wish to include other specific duties, such as general food shopping, ironing, holidaying with the family or dealing with issues relating to special needs or medical conditions. In any event, all duties should be laid down in a written contract of employment. See the website, and Appendix 1, pages 283–91.

QUALIFICATIONS

Nanny qualifications could fill an entire book in themselves. It's amazing the number of parents who breathe a sigh of relief at knowing a girl is 'qualified' without stopping to wonder what she has actually studied, where and how, and what grade she achieved. A really good nanny should come to an interview with her certificates to prove the distinctions her CV mentions. Any candidate who claims to be qualified but can't produce the paperwork should be treated as unqualified. Similarly, any candidate who has been awarded startlingly low grades should be questioned carefully about her commitment to the profession.

COST

Unlike a childminder, your nanny is your employee and you will have to pay her salary deducting tax and National Insurance contributions at source – in other words, you pay her tax and NI contributions out of your own taxed income, which for many families not only seems a tad unfair but can be financially crippling. At the time of writing, a number of provisions are in place to reduce this tax burden such as voucher schemes and tax credits (see Appendix 2, pages 295–8, and website for details) but these are generally seen as not going far enough for the average working parent.

If the cost puts you off the idea of employing a nanny, don't dismiss it entirely until you have considered nannysharing (see Chapter 5), an increasingly popular option for families in which money doesn't grow on trees.

Live-in nannies can expect to earn, on average:

- £350 a week (net) in central London
- £260–300 a week (net) elsewhere

Daily nannies can expect to earn, on average:

- £450–£550 a week (net) in central London
- £350–400 a week (net) elsewhere

These figures may vary greatly even across a single city or area, and will go up or down in proportion to a nanny's qualifications, experience and even the marketplace and economic climate. An experienced nanny will usually be happy to let you know her salary expectations, and although you should specify a gross salary in her contract, the figure she will give you is likely to be net of tax and National Insurance contributions. This is something I find it hard to explain to new employers, who themselves receive a gross salary and are mostly not even aware of their net hourly rate. Nannying is probably the only profession where salaries are quoted net. I can only put this down to the fact that a lot of parents have historically employed nannies without paying their tax, and as this has become less common, nannies have not completely adapted their own expectations.

To work out your projected total cost, contact one of the nanny payroll companies (see Resources, page 324); they also offer general advice on contracts and can provide specific advice on more complex issues, such as nannysharing.

REGISTERED NANNIES

While childminders and nurseries must be registered, nannies need not. They can, however, register on the voluntary part of the Ofsted Childcare Register (OCR). There are advantages in registering to parents and nannies.

- If you use a registered nanny and your employer operates a childcare voucher scheme you can save tax and National Insurance on a proportion of her weekly salary.
- Registration shows that a nanny is deemed suitable by Ofsted to work with children.
- It increases the nanny's professional status.

As well as knowledge of the common core skills, a nanny should have a first-aid certificate and public liability insurance. The cost of registration includes that of CRB disclosure (police check) and this will be carried out even if your nanny has received a clear police check the previous week. The registration fee is usually paid by the parents, who stand to gain financially, although some nannies looking for new positions are already registered. Registration may take 12–16 weeks to complete.

REGISTRATION PROCEDURE

A nanny must apply on the Ofsted website. Ofsted will write to her to let her know that they have received the application. The letter will include details on how to:

- obtain an enhanced CRB disclosure
- get identity, and other information checked
- pay the application fee

Ofsted will assess the nanny's suitability by considering the information on the application form and CRB disclosure.

If the nanny has lived abroad in the past three years the CRB will make use of reciprocal arrangements that allow it to check on criminal history overseas. Where there is no such arrangement, Ofsted will normally require the nanny to provide some extra evidence of suitability, which may include:

- a certificate of good conduct from the embassy of the country in which the nanny lived, accompanied where necessary by a certified translation into English
- a reference from someone of standing in the country in which the nanny lived, such as a doctor or lawyer
- evidence to support any work permit
- references from past employers

A nanny can be refused if she has already been disqualified, is unsuitable, fails to pay the fee, does not agree to the requirements of the register or lives with someone who is disqualified. She has the right to object to the refusal.

Once the nanny has been granted registration a certificate is issued. This is proof that the nanny is registered on the voluntary part of the Childcare Register and she must show the certificate to parents on request.

Amanda Coxen at Tinies Childcare has doubts about the voluntary registration system: 'We are very disappointed with the OCR. Very few of our childcarers are registered and those who are have only done so in order that their employers can make use of childcare vouchers.'

For more details on the skills nannies should have before registering with the Ofsted Childcare Register, and a list of recommended qualifications and where to get them, see the Ofsted website: www.ofsted.gov.uk. This is an area that has been constantly under review and it is worth checking the up-to-date position before making any decisions.

HOURS

A live-in nanny can expect to work a 12-hour day, five days a week, but a daily nanny will generally work 10–11 hours per day, the rationale being that she needs time to get to and from work. You can ask a daily nanny to work 12 hours and she may be glad of the extra cash, but at the end of the day you should consider the interests of your children, who will benefit much more from a nanny who has had a good night's sleep! In the case of a live-out nanny, allow for handover time when you define the hours of work, so that she has a few minutes on arrival and departure to talk to you about plans for the day and to report back.

PROS

- Flexibility: a nanny's hours and duties are tailored to suit your needs and lifestyle rather than those of an institution.
- She can care for all your children in the one setting.
- Your child remains in your home (unless it's a nannyshare, in which case you may alternate homes or use the other home as a base) so less settling-in is required.
- You don't need to bring your child home and get her ready for bed every day: she will be bathed and in her pyjamas by the time you get back from work.
- Your baby will still be looked after if he is ill.
- Voluntary Ofsted registration is available, saving you money on tax and National Insurance.

CONS

- Cost: this is the most expensive childcare option.
- You're responsible for deducting tax and National Insurance from her pay, which, as well as making this option expensive, is a time-consuming and complex procedure.
- CRB checks and Ofsted registration can take many weeks.
- There is no compulsory registration for nannies so it is still an unregulated market.
- Nannies may not be trained or qualified and they work alone, which involves trust on your part.
- Nannies in their early twenties may not (in your view) necessarily be mature enough to cope with the demands of several small children, even when they are qualified.

- If your nanny is ill, you either have to take time off work at the last minute, or bring in a temporary nanny at extra expense.
- Much hangs on your personal relationship with a nanny: it needs plenty of attention if you are to get the best out of her.
- If the children of another family come to your house you'll need to check with your household insurer that you are covered for any accidents that may occur.

TYPICAL DAY

What happens in a nanny's day will vary hugely, depending on the ages and number of children she is looking after, whether you live in a town or rural area, what activities are available locally and, most importantly, what you want her to do with your children all day. Some parents are particularly keen for their children to be out and about socialising; others rate regular meals and naps in the home environment above all else and like to keep outings and disruption of routine to a minimum. When you interview your nanny, listen to what ideas she has about filling her day, and discuss how much or how little socialising you want to be involved.

A nanny will usually arrive when your children are still in their pyjamas, and her first job will be to get them dressed and breakfasted. Mornings are often the time for playgroups, music groups and organised entertainment; discuss with your nanny which you would like your child to join. If she isn't familiar with the area you may be able to ask the agency to put her in touch with other nannies or to provide her with some ideas. After lunch and a nap (if applicable), afternoon activities might consist of some one-to-one play with the nanny, working on developing gross and fine motor skills, language, memory and numbers through puzzles, games, art and sensory play. Most nannies also like to spend time with children outdoors, using up their energy at the local park or playground. Playdates, where other nannies or mothers bring their children to play with yours at your house, or vice versa, are usually an important part of a nanny's week, but you are within your rights to set limits on these to make sure you are getting the most from the one-to-one care you have chosen. Your nanny will cook your children's tea and usually bath them, so you can spend quality time with them when you get home. During the last few minutes of the day, she should tell you what has happened, any important developments or plans for the rest of the week. She should also have filled in her nanny diary (see example below), recording the day's events: it will provide not only a useful record for parents but a souvenir for children when they are older.

SAMPLE FROM A NANNY'S DIARY – CARING FOR A TWO-YEAR-OLD

23 September 2009

Breakfast Weetabix and toast with butter, half an apple
Morning Music class
Lunch Cottage pie with carrots and peas, yoghurt, water
Nap 1.30 p.m.–3 p.m.
Afternoon Walked to park and library – new library books on

toy box in playroom, came home and did puzzles, 30 mins CBeebies

Tea Pasta with broccoli and pesto, banana custard

Money Carrots – 80p from kitty

Notes Only one dirty nappy – used potty three times! New words – 'monkey' and 'spider'. Have invited Felix to play tomorrow morning, have made extra cottage pie and put it in freezer.

This is a very general picture of how your nanny may spend her day, and doesn't take into account school and nursery runs or household chores that may be covered by your contract with her.

FINDING A NANNY

The best time to begin the search for a nanny is around eight weeks before you need her to start. This will give you plenty of time to register with agencies and post ads on the Internet and in magazines or newspapers, while giving any prospective candidate time to work out her notice (usually a month). However, many families need an immediate start – for example, if their existing nanny leaves suddenly, or if the parent who is usually in charge becomes incapacitated. Most agencies and websites can help you find a nanny at short notice.

You may have an idea of your ideal nanny candidate, perhaps formed through meeting other nannies, hearing about other people's experiences, or watching *Mary Poppins* too often, but the fact is, you may never meet that perfect match. If you have to go back to work and a nanny is your chosen option, you may find yourself having to settle for someone less wonderful than you anticipated. Having said that, there are certain standard requirements for personality that continue to be at the top of the list for parents:

- cheerful
- neat and organised
- good sense of humour
- punctual, trustworthy and reliable
- safety-conscious
- polite
- good fun
- child-loving and affectionate

In a nutshell, you are looking for someone who is technically competent with a sunny disposition and will win your and your children's respect and affection.

You may have to compromise, most commonly, on:

- intelligence (don't look for A levels on the CV!)
- perfect written and spoken English
- arts and crafts/sporting activities (many nannies tend to steer one way or the other)
- cooking skills (many nannies live with their parents and need guidance in the kitchen)
- ability to deal with different age-groups at once

Before starting the search, decide the following issues, which any agency will want to know about and will be important if you decide to draft an ad:

- whether you want a live-in or daily nanny – a live-in candidate won't share a room with a child, and will usually be looking for her own bathroom or a shared bathroom with the children. More and more live-in nannies are looking for full accommodation with separate entrance, but the state of the UK economy will usually dictate how realistic that idea is!
- what duties you wish the nanny to perform – an agency should be able to help you ascertain what is and is not reasonable to ask. See also Duties, page 70
- what hours you will need the nanny to work – no more than a 12-hour day for a live-in nanny, and up to 11 for a live-out nanny
- whether you would be happy for a nanny to bring her own baby or child to work with her – this will open up a raft of possibilities and in my experience is a great option, especially for single children who need company. However, a nanny with children of her own, whether or not she brings them to work with her, may be more limited as regards finish times: she will want to get home and spend some time with her own family
- whether you have any special requirements, such as the nanny's need to speak a language other than English – it's becoming increasingly common for parents to look for bilingual nannies
- whether you want your nanny to babysit/go on holiday with you. Babysitting may be negotiated as part of a job

offer or paid separately. Depending on their personal circumstances, nannies vary greatly in their keenness to take on such extra work

- whether your nanny should like pets
- whether she needs to be a driver
- whether she needs to own a car (think about parking permits)
- whether she needs to have experience of children with special needs (see Appendix 3, pages 301–3)

USING AN AGENCY

There are hundreds of nanny agencies throughout the UK, of varying standards. Most charge a one-off introduction fee in the event that you hire one of their candidates. Using an agency can give parents a sense of security but, like the nanny market, the agencies are relatively unregulated. Corners are cut, short-cuts are taken and children's lives and well-being are at stake. Until there is more regulation of agencies, all parents should go into professional recruitment with their eyes open. Read this section carefully before you use a nanny agency, and pay particular attention to the nightmare scenario that plays out in Meghan's story (page 97).

THE PROS OF USING AN AGENCY

The upside is that they have access potentially to many more girls than you will attract by advertising privately, and their experience in interviewing candidates can be comforting to a first-time employer. Most agencies will have an alert system to warn them about unsuitable candidates, protecting you from those who may advertise their services privately. Agencies usually offer you a standard contract, help with negotiating salary and terms, and support throughout the placement.

THE CONS OF USING AN AGENCY

The downside is that interviewing and vetting a nanny is not rocket science, and you can achieve the same peace of mind yourself through common sense and carrying out your own background checks. In my view an agency's main value lies in the pool of candidates and time-saving rather than any particular skill in recruitment technique. (And I say that as an agent.) Different agencies also have different fee structures. Some charge according to how many days per week the nanny will work, and others a multiple of the nanny's salary. I have always felt there is a slight conflict of interest with the latter system, as it can lead to agencies pushing clients into paying over the odds in terms of salary in order to boost turnover. Shop around with that in mind.

TOP TIPS FOR USING AN AGENCY

- Many agencies advertise in the same magazines and on the same websites that you will, and you may be sent CVs of candidates you have already met online or through other means. If this happens, make sure you inform the agency immediately so that you don't fall foul of their terms of business and get billed for a nanny you already knew.

- If you do use an agency, don't be afraid to ask detailed questions about candidates they send you. Why did she leave her last job? Which referees has the agency spoken to personally? Did any say anything negative about her? Make sure you get your money's worth and read the small print – many a refund procedure in the terms of business is not what it seems.

- Ask specifically if the agency or anyone at the agency is aware of anything about the candidate that has not been disclosed on the CV or in conversations with you.

- Check that the CV sent to you by the agency and the version the nanny gives you tell the same story. Agencies have been known to produce convenient summaries of CVs that don't disclose the full picture, omitting temporary and unsuccessful positions.

- Communicate, be specific in your requirements, report back after interviews and ask for feedback from candidates, who are likely to have been more than frank with any recruitment consultant.

- Look at the fee structure to make sure you are getting a good deal. Shop around rather than paying an unreasonable finder's fee for a candidate who may have registered at several local agencies.

- Even the best agencies, at the end of the day, are limited in how far they can control their 'product', i.e. the candidates. Carefully vetted and competent nannies occasionally fail to appear for interviews or let families down at the last minute. If this happens to you, don't reject the agency straight away as what has happened may have been beyond their control. The important thing is how they deal with the problem: whether they are apologetic and sympathetic, or whether you feel brushed off. In the latter instance, it would be perfectly reasonable to assume that you might do better going elsewhere.

ADVERTISING FOR A NANNY YOURSELF

If you decide not to use an agency, or want to start by doing some homework yourself and possibly save money in the process, you have a number of options:

- advertising in a magazine or local paper
- advertising in your local library
- advertising on a school notice board
- advertising on the Internet on a childcare-recruitment website (see Resources, pages 323–4)

TOP TIPS FOR DIY NANNY RECRUITMENT

- Make the job sound irresistible to ensure that the maximum number of good candidates apply – but don't promise what you can't deliver, or be unrealistic about the salary or hours: 'Full-time sole-charge live-in nanny sought for children aged 2 and 4, excellent salary and benefits for right candidate, separate accommodation in basement flat with shared garden.'

- Ask for slightly more than you strictly need in terms of experience and level of English, and you will limit the number of responses to something below the thousands. The fact is that, although it is traditionally the source of good Australasian childcare, www.gumtree.com has become a favourite with non-English-speaking Central Europeans who imagine that having a younger brother back home in Bucharest entitles them to £350 per week as a live-in nanny in Surrey. Demand native English or equivalent, good experience and checkable English-language references, or you will be deluged: 'Must be native English speaker and confident driver with at least 2 years' childcare experience in the UK and checkable written references, qualifications preferred.'

- Ask respondents to email a CV in the first instance so you can see at a glance whether they are good enough on paper to merit an interview.

- If hundreds of unsuitables present themselves in your inbox (or no candidates at all), go back to the website and amend the advert – changing it should cost you nothing.

- Check references very thoroughly indeed. Don't rely on written references alone, but speak to as many previous employers as you can, and ask them detailed questions (see page 95 for detailed guidelines on taking up references).

NETWORKING FOR A NANNY

Lots of parents find nannies through friends, so don't underestimate the power of the playground when it comes to making good childcare contacts. Many a deal is done at the school gate, and it's a favourite hunting ground for the celebrity sector! Happy nannies are unlikely to leave their employers, of course, but when offered double their money, health club membership and a car of their own some find it hard to resist. The moral of the story must be to limit the amount of time your nanny is allowed to spend on the school run . . .

CHOOSING CANDIDATES TO INTERVIEW

Once you have the CVs in front of you, whether through an agency or otherwise, you may be none the wiser. On paper, an experienced and qualified nanny may look impressive, but in person may lack the certain something that makes you click with her and feel happy about handing over your children to her care. Similarly, an apparently under-experienced young Polish girl may surprise you with her enthusiasm and resourcefulness. So, choosing between candidates is a tricky business and I would advise interviewing as many as possible so you don't miss out on that magic connection.

There are some general skills and attributes to look for. A good nanny should:

➤ either be qualified or at least have plenty of experience of caring for children of your children's age

- be able to plan and arrange safe, fun activities and learning opportunities
- know how to plan and prepare healthy meals (although there are plenty of parents who are prepared to compromise on this if she is happy to use a good recipe book)
- have first-aid training (if not, send her on a course)
- have driving experience if required
- have a genuine interest in children as individuals, and be interested in their development as well as having fun with them
- have a confident, warm and positive personality
- have experience of working with children of various ages, in a variety of different settings
- have good checkable references, preferably written, with phone and email contact details
- have a good attendance record

So while you are looking through the CVs:

- make a shortlist of potential nannies from applications received
- talk to each selected applicant on the phone (usually an agency will arrange for them to call you)
- set up interview appointments, allowing at least one hour for each applicant and some thinking time afterwards, and reminding them to bring *copies* of their CV and references, as well as ID, driving licence and certificates, and preferably a photo
- prepare a list of questions and put them to each applicant (see below)

- take notes at each interview to remind you of their answers

INTERVIEWING CANDIDATES

It helps to be organised about the interview process. Keep a file for all the CVs, photos, references and accompanying documents of the candidates you are considering, and keep your notes in it to remind you of your impressions. It's amazing how quickly you forget when you are seeing several girls at a time. Also, keep a record of the source of the candidate, name of the agency, if relevant, and date sent. This will clear up any confusion that may arise over who sent you the details first, and may avoid problems with several agencies claiming to have sent you the same candidate. Keep copies of all relevant emails for your own records.

Be ready for your candidate – she may arrive early in her keenness to give a good impression. You don't need to spend hours tidying up (though clearing enough space on the sofa so she can sit down is a good idea). Consider whether you want your children to be there during the interview: will they get in the way or would you like to see how she interacts with them and what they think of her? Many seasoned interviewers run a two-stage process, meeting a nanny alone for the first interview and inviting the best candidates back for a second interview and to meet the children. Sometimes the father isn't present at the first round.

At the interview think about asking the following questions but don't feel you have to stick rigidly to the script: you will probably find that conversation flows quite naturally and you won't need to consult this list.

1. What qualifications or experience does she have?
2. What does she like most about being a nanny? *(Children!)*
3. Are there any aspects of the job that she doesn't like?
4. How long has she been a nanny and why did she choose it as a career?
5. How did she get on with the children in her last job?
6. How did she get on with the parents in previous jobs?
7. What difficulties has she experienced with parents/children in live-in positions? How were these resolved?
8. What activities would she do with children aged X and Y?
9. What might a typical day be like for your children?
10. Does she have any experience of toilet training?
11. What behaviour/developmental stages would she expect from a [6–10-month-old and a two-year-old]?
12. How would she stimulate their development?
13. What would she do if:
    (a) the toddler was at nursery and the baby was taken seriously ill?
    (b) the children are playing in the garden and the baby needed a nappy change?
    (c) at bath time she found a bruise/injury on one of the children that you were not previously aware of?
    (d) she found herself getting stressed by her job?
14. What sort of meals would she prepare for them?
15. Does she have a current first-aid certificate? Can she deal with/has she ever dealt with a first-aid emergency?
16. What are her views on discipline and manners? She should have her own ideas, not just follow your lead.
17. Is her own social life important to her in her work? Does she have a particular nanny friend she is inseparable from?

How old are the children the other nanny looks after? Would they make suitable playmates for yours?

18. How is her health? Any issues that might affect her work in any way? How many days off sick in her previous position? (Remember that nursery staff are absent more frequently than nannies.)
19. Is she generally clean and tidy around the house?
20. What is she getting paid in her current job?
21. Does her employer know she is looking for work?
22. Why is her current job ending?
23. What are her long-term plans? (You should be able to gauge whether nannying is her chosen career or a stop-gap.)
24. Does she have any questions?

Interviewing is a two-way process. Give her the chance to ask you questions and make sure you tell her:

1. All about your children – their likes and dislikes, their personalities, funny ways, etc.
2. Your views on discipline: would she feel happy following your procedures?
3. Your views on television, videos, sweets and other treats.
4. Your requirements regarding activities – if it is important that your child continues to attend a particular playgroup, for example.
5. Your requirements regarding any additional duties, such as washing and ironing, occasional grocery shopping, running errands to the dry-cleaner, the post office, etc.
6. Your work schedule, the exact hours she will be needed,

any babysitting or holiday work, and whether you will be at home for any of the time she is working.

7. The exact salary, whether it's a daily or hourly rate, whether gross or net, whether you will pay for her petrol/parking permit/car insurance, and any perks like gym membership, extra holiday, etc.
8. With holiday in particular, discuss any holidays you or she may have already planned, and what your ongoing requirements are regarding taking holiday within school holiday times.
9. How long you will need a nanny for – if your youngest is starting school in September, be honest about your expectations; will you want to bring another family in as a share?

WHAT NOT TO ASK

There is a lot of paranoia around what you can and can't ask a candidate, and this may reach such an extreme that a parent will be walking on eggshells during an interview. You can compensate for this in tell-it-like-it is style when dealing with the agency direct. I have had clients specify that their nanny needs to be over twenty-five, with five years' childcare experience, Catholic, no bigger than a size fourteen, but not too pretty . . . and I am often at pains to explain that I can't list such requirements on the advert. Generally parents think they can be honest with an agency and careful with the nanny, but it does help to understand a little about why anti-discrimination legislation (see website for full details) has been introduced.

The point is that any candidate should be judged on his or her ability to do the job in question. Although a parent may be absolutely convinced that anything less than five years' sole-charge nanny experience is unacceptable, I feel I need to disabuse them of this conviction for their own benefit. For a start, by opening the gates to nannies of all ages, sizes and religious persuasions they will be more likely to find the right person, and by closing them they will certainly miss out on some fabulous nannies.

The general rule is that at interview you shouldn't ask about any issue that directly or indirectly relates to age, race, sex, marital status, disability, religion or sexual orientation. Take care when you are dealing with an obese candidate: their weight gain may have been caused by a disability. However, you are entitled to ask questions that genuinely relate to someone's ability to do the job. For example, if it involves working on Saturday and your candidate is devoutly Jewish then you would be entitled to ask how it will fit with their religious practices.

If all this seems like a minefield, think less about rules and more about approaching all issues with sensitivity and common sense; show willingness to discuss solutions; avoiding making assumptions and stereotyping.

CHILDREN WITH SPECIAL NEEDS

As well as all the usual considerations involved in choosing a nanny, you may also need to think about questions like:

- Does the nanny have experience in looking after a child with a similar disability, and if not, would they be happy for you to show them what's needed?
- How much specialist care does your child need and is appropriate training available locally?

- Does your child have therapy or appointments that they need to go to in the time they will be cared for, and can your nanny take your child to them?
- Does the nanny need specialist training or equipment? Does she have to have specific training to give medication? As a parent, you'll be shown how to do this by your doctor, a nurse or health visitor. You can ask the same person to give this training to your child's new nanny.

See also Appendix 3, pages 301–3.

SECOND INTERVIEWS

If you are convinced you have found Mary Poppins, feel free to offer her the job there and then, but most people prefer to sleep on it and/or to invite the candidate back for a second interview. If you are sure you would like to see her again, make the arrangement at the interview so that she knows you want to take things further. It sometimes happens that during the busy parents' thinking process, a nanny can be offered another job, which she accepts. If she knows you are interested and is interested herself, she will wait until you have made a decision.

Many people like to invite their prospective nanny back for a second interview (although there is no rule saying you must), perhaps to meet the spouse and children. This can be a good opportunity to clarify the details of the children's daily routines and the nanny's duties, show her round the house, get to know her a little better and to watch how she interacts with the children. I always recommend that my clients take plenty of time over the second interview, maybe getting the candidate in for a couple of hours to play with the children, and pay her for her time. If you are about to incur a vast agency fee, not to mention the personal commitment of giving a virtual stranger sole charge of your children, you should take as much time as you need to be 110 per cent sure about it.

Either at the second interview or whenever you offer her the position, make sure your new nanny knows:

- her salary, with details about tax and National Insurance arrangements, including overtime and babysitting rates and how payment will be made, monthly or weekly, by cheque or directly into a bank account, etc.
- exactly when you want her to start, date and time, allowing for any overlap and her notice period
- exact holiday entitlement and sick pay – most parents pay the nanny when she is sick, but don't expect this to happen very often
- the length of the probationary period, if any (usually this is built into the contract and will involve one week's notice for the first month on either side). Think carefully about announcing a probationary period: it can make a nanny feel too insecure to take the job. The fact is that if things don't work out, they don't work out, whether you agree a trial month or not

CHECKING REFERENCES

I cannot emphasise strongly enough the importance of checking references thoroughly. Whether recruiting myself or on behalf of clients, I ask candidates to bring written references with up-to-date contact details, then try to contact as many of the referees as possible by phone. Ironically, although employing a nanny could be said to amount to handing over your most precious possession to a complete stranger, a shocking number of parents don't give proper time and thought to this process.

Samantha Kelly, of Kids Matter, in Leicestershire, is a real detective when it comes to reference checking: 'We uncovered a forged reference from a nanny this spring. The nanny had given false telephone numbers of friends to act as her ex-employers if anyone called. She had also changed the content of the written reference. This nanny was registered with 10 agencies in London and we were the only agency that spotted this.'

Here are the most common reasons why parents fail to check references by phone.

- ➤ They assume (not unreasonably) that the agency has done a thorough job.
- ➤ They have seen good enough written references.
- ➤ They are told the employers have moved or changed numbers.
- ➤ They don't have enough time and it slips off the end of the to-do list.

If you are looking independently for a nanny for your children, you have every reason to leave no stone unturned in the recruitment process. Agencies, however, do not always accord the same importance as you would to collecting references, and will generally promise only that they have spoken to 'at least two' referees. If a referee gives a cautious recommendation, the agency may still put forward the candidate if no childcare issue is involved, regardless of questions about the candidate's honesty. The business of agencies is to make money through maximising the number of placements, and sometimes means that they fail to pass on a negative comment in a reference if they feel it is not strictly relevant.

I was told Meghan's story by a client whom I had advised not to employ a particular candidate another agency had put forward. I had met the nanny and decided against sending her to clients because her previous employers had alleged dishonesty relating to absence from work, which would have put me off employing her to look after my children (a measure I still use to judge the suitability of candidates today). It is possibly the worst story I have ever heard direct so please don't imagine that this experience is by any means common. The story that follows it will reassure you if Meghan's gives you the jitters.

Meghan had been a regular client of mine for some years but, not unreasonably, would register with a number of agencies when she was looking for childcare. Another London agency sent her the details of an attractive, well-spoken and seemingly very experienced nanny in her late twenties. Assuming the agency had completed the usual background checks, Meghan offered her the job on the spot. At this point she contacted me to let me know she was no longer looking. I happened to ask the name of the nanny.

She turned out to be Kerry, a candidate whose unsuitability I had discussed with the other agency. Her background checks had revealed that previous employers had despaired at her frequent and unexplained absences from work, and that on one occasion it had emerged that Kerry was interviewing for other positions while claiming to be in Yorkshire visiting her sick mother. When Meghan went back to the other agency to voice her concerns, they spoke at length about the importance of childcare standards over anything else, and assured Meghan that, in their investigations into Kerry's employment history, no childcare issue had emerged to give them cause for concern.

To cut a long story short, Kerry lasted precisely two weeks with Meghan – and only two days of that period with sole charge. On the first day, she failed to turn up, claiming that on her return from holiday her bag had been lost at the airport. On the second day, a number of worrying incidents caused alarm bells to ring: misleading diary entries, toddlers left unsupervised at play, and a minor fire in the kitchen brought her employment to a premature halt.

On further investigation, Meghan then noticed that the CV the agency had sent differed quite considerably from the one Kerry had handed to her at the interview. There were significant anomalies in dates and job descriptions, as if the agency had ironed out the rough spots and made the picture more conveniently palatable.

Fortunately the agency in question honoured their contract and provided Meghan with a replacement for Kerry, but by then the children were so traumatised by their experiences that Meghan decided to hand in her notice at work. The moral of that story is – as illustrated – check the references.

Annabel's story is quite different:

I have had six or seven girls come to work for me through various agencies. In each case, as well as asking the agency which referees they had spoken to and what they had said, I used the numbers I was given to contact the two most recent employers. I always asked these employers which of the previous ones they had spoken to when they first recruited the childcarer in question. I was pleasantly surprised to find that not only had I been sent details of girls whose backgrounds checked out more or less perfectly, but also that the reports from the agency matched exactly what the recent employers told me they had heard when checking the references themselves. I know that some agencies are possibly more lax than others on this, but once this agency had won my trust I resolved never to go anywhere else and I recommend them to my friends. My advice is always to ask around when it comes to using an agency. Don't just do a Google search.

TOP TIPS FOR REFERENCE CHECKING

I have emphasised the importance of checking references by phone, but when you make the call, it's vital to extract all relevant information from the referee in whatever limited time you have. Here are some tips.

- Check that it's a convenient time to talk, and if it isn't, suggest that you ring back another time. Don't rely on them calling you.
- Check that you are speaking to the right person – first, that they are one of the parents, and second, that this parent had enough contact with the nanny to give a proper opinion of her. Remember that, in some cases, this will be the father.
- Have a pen and paper handy so you can take notes: you

may not remember everything and will need to discuss what you are told with your partner.

- Ask plenty of open questions to make sure they have the opportunity to elaborate on your points. In particular, in case your conversation is cut short, ask for a summary of the best and worst aspects of the candidate as early on as possible.
- Emphasise the confidentiality of your conversation. The referee is likely to be a lot more candid on the phone than in a written reference, but will need your reassurance that what he/she says will not be passed on to the candidate in question.

Questions for referees

There are no hard and fast rules about what to ask a referee on the phone but here is a list of basic questions to which you should get answers before employing anyone. You may find the agency you use can provide you with a list of their questions and the referees' answers, especially if they have only managed to make contact by email, for example, but check that all these points have been covered.

1. When did the candidate work for you?
2. In what exact capacity?
3. Did she have sole charge, and if so how much?
4. What were the ages of the children in her care?
5. What were her duties and how flexible was she about them?
6. Was she cheerful and pleasant to have around?
7. How would you rate her honesty and trustworthiness?

8. How would you rate her punctuality?
9. Was she ever off sick?
10. (If applicable) How would you rate her driving?
11. How well did she get on with the children?
12. How well did she get on with you [and your partner]?
13. How would you rate her cooking skills?
14. How creative/artistic was she?
15. Did she take direction well?
16. Could she use her initiative?
17. Did she organise appropriate activities for the ages of the children, including developmental work, art and messy play?
18. What were the circumstances of her leaving?
19. Would you re-employ her? If not, why not?
20. Any other comments? Any reservations about recommending her?

REFERENCES AND CONFIDENTIALITY

A lot has been made in the press over the last few years of the issue of confidentiality. A nanny wants to know what has been said about her by previous employers and data-protection rules give her the right to know that. However, an agency is not obliged to divulge the *source* of any reference, or to give away any information that might reveal their identity. In a nutshell, you should be able to rely on anything you say in a reference being kept confidential from the subject. If necessary, you can quote this rule when speaking to referees – in certain cases, it may make them a lot more forthcoming!

THE NEW NANNY STARTS WORK

Once your preferred candidate has accepted the job, you should draw up a written contract (see page 107 for essential contract terms, Appendix 1, pages 283–91, and the website for more advice on contracts). You should produce two copies of the contract, both of which should be signed by both the nanny and you as the employer, then keep one copy each.

Most parents like there to be a handover period, varying between a day and a month, either with Mum (or Dad) or the previous nanny, when she can learn the route for the school run and how the washing-machine works, so that you and she are relaxed and confident when the day comes for you to leave your children in her sole charge. It may sound obvious, but make sure she knows what to call you, any children's nicknames and how she should address other family members. Give her a list of house rules: no shoes upstairs, dog not allowed in bedrooms, etc.

Tinies Childcare has an excellent checklist for nanny induction on their website, which I have reproduced here with their kind permission:

Your children

1. What are their likes and dislikes?

- Favourite toys, books and characters
- Special soft toy friends or comforters
- Any allergies or regular medications – how and when to administer
- Food – what are their favourite dishes and what do you prefer them to eat?

- Who are their nearest and dearest – grandparents, cousins, aunties, uncles and friends?

2. Go through:

- routines (sleep, play, bathtime, eating)
- approach to discipline
- television
- taking telephone messages and making calls
- dealing with people who come to the door
- petty cash/expenses
- nanny diary – how will you correspond with each other at the start and end of the day?

General

1. Around the house:

- Kitchen – how does the cooker/washing-machine/microwave work?
- Where do you keep your vacuum cleaner and cleaning products?
- Where is your first-aid kit and medicine?
- Where is your sewing box?
- Locking-up procedures – alarm codes
- If the nanny is live-in, does she need a shelf for her own food, etc.?

2. Introduce your nanny to your:

- neighbours
- playgroups, swimming classes, NCT, etc.
- children's teachers and play workers

- children's friends, their carers and parents
- any other people who are important to your family

3. Prepare a contact list.

- Phone numbers, to include parents' work and mobiles, neighbours, school, doctors, grandparents, friends.
- Will your nanny always be able to contact you at work?

4. Equipment check and demonstrations.

- Car seats, correctly fitted into car (check with her car and yours).
- Pushchairs, buggies and high-chairs – give demonstrations in how to collapse them.
- Tour of the local area: parks, library, shops, swimming-pools, schools, playgroups, doctors, hospital.

THE SOLE-CHARGE QUESTION

Nannies love sole charge, and it's often the first stipulation they make on registering with an agency. They all have a nightmare story about the perils of working with Mum at home, and have usually told all their friends, so the nightmare gets magnified and embellished to the point at which it can be almost impossible to find a nanny to work alongside you in the home. If you are looking for a sole-charge nanny, you will have the pick of the bunch. If you aren't, there are a few points to consider at the recruitment stage and once you have your nanny in place.

- Be honest in your advert or with the agency – there is no point in advertising a position as sole charge if you are going to work from home even one day a week. You will end up wasting your time interviewing candidates who are of the over-my-dead-body persuasion when it comes to shared-charge work.
- At interview, be specific about the days and times you are likely to be around and how involved you want to be with the children. If you are going to be holed up in your home office all day, only sneaking into the kitchen for a cup of tea when nanny and kids are out, say so – a reasonable candidate is likely to see that this is just as good as sole charge.
- Make sure that you and your nanny agree very clear rules and boundaries about such issues as feeding and discipline. Many nannies complain that a shared-charge situation can lead to parents walking in and handing out biscuits to children who are about to have lunch, or undermining a disciplinary decision they don't agree with. These things are very easy to do, and a good nanny is very easy to lose!
- When your nanny starts work, let her have as much sole charge as possible so that she can assert her authority over the children. If you are around, defer to your nanny when the children come running for a second opinion. Make sure there is no doubt in your children's mind about who is in charge. As soon as children see a loophole in authority they will use it, and this can make a nanny's job very difficult.

Amanda writes:

> *When my second baby was born, I kept my nanny, Rachel, on through my maternity leave – nearly six months of shared charge for her, and me being tired and irritable. I think she found it very hard at first, suddenly having me around and my little boy playing us off against each other. I could see that she was feeling out of control and we sat down and had a chat about it. It was a strange situation, really. She was used to running the show while I went to work, and now here I was getting in the way and undermining her authority (unintentionally) with Josh. I just wanted to be at home and be around the house but I felt that I wasn't really welcome, and wasn't free to do what I wanted. Luckily, we get on well enough and communicate well enough to get through these things, and we were able to come up with a plan to deal with the problem that suited both of us. Basically it involved Rachel being very organised about planning activities, and me being consistent and predictable, and, yes, more absent than I wanted to be. It sounds so boring but boundaries and rules are a very good thing when it comes to childcare!*

YOUR RESPONSIBILITIES AS AN EMPLOYER

You may feel relieved that the search is finally over, but shaking hands and agreeing to hire your new nanny is just the beginning. Keeping her happy and motivated will be a vital element of your relationship. As well as being a mother and wife at home, and an employee in your own workplace, you are now an employer, which brings with it a host of obligations, legal and personal, some of which may be news to you.

Contract of employment It is a legal requirement to provide your nanny with a written contract of employment. By law, she is entitled to a written statement setting out the main particulars of her employment within two months of starting work. Most agencies can provide you with a specimen contract (see also Appendix 1, pages 283–91, and the website).

Statutory employment rights A number of statutory rights apply to employees as soon as they start work. These rights exist regardless of the contract. The law protects your nanny against unlawful deductions from wages, against adverse treatment on grounds of sex, race, sexual orientation, religion and religious belief, age or disability, and against dismissal for seeking to enforce statutory employment rights. Others, such as the right to make a general complaint of unfair dismissal, apply on completion of a qualifying period of service.

Contractual rights and obligations You should include in the employment contract the following points, some of which are legal requirements for any employment contract and some of which make good sense in the context of employing a nanny:

- your name and address and your nanny's name and address
- the job description: what you expect the nanny to do (useful to attach a detailed schedule)
- her hours and place of work, and whether travel is expected

- whether babysitting is included
- arrangements for payment for petrol, and car insurance
- use of telephone
- dismissal and grievance procedures (which sounds formal and complicated, but all it means is outlining what she should do if she has a problem and what she can expect you to do if you have a problem)
- probationary period, if any
- salary (net or gross, how much, when and how paid) and when salary reviews will happen
- holiday arrangements
- sick-pay entitlements
- notice period
- confirmation of pension arrangements, including the effect, if any, on the state earnings-related pension scheme
- confirmation that no collective agreements affect the employment (they tend to exist in large, often unionised workforces, so all you are required to say is that none exists for your nanny)

Pay Your nanny's pay will depend on the type of job (live-in or live-out), the hours, the number of children to be cared for, her qualifications and experience, and the area in which you live. Nannies are covered by the national minimum wage and, as your nanny's employer, you are responsible for paying her tax and National Insurance contributions (NICs) as well as your NICs as employer. Although nannies have a peculiar habit of looking for a particular level of net pay, it is advisable to quote your nanny's salary as a gross figure in your contract to limit your liability to tax and NICs. Subject to keeping up with the national minimum wage, you are not under any obligation to increase your nanny's salary, but it is good practice to offer an annual salary review.

Tax and NICs Nannies cannot be self-employed, and the old loophole that enabled you to set up your nanny as a company and save tax that way has long been closed. You must deduct employee tax and NICs from your nanny's pay at source, unless you are paying less than the lower earnings limit. This must be done through the HMRC PAYE (Pay As You Earn) scheme. If you are paying your nanny less than the lower earnings limit you will not need to make payments on her behalf, but she can still pay voluntary NICs; you will also have to make employer NICs. See Resources, pages 313–32, for contact details of payroll companies who can organise this for you, and the website for further information.

Insurance When you employ a nanny it is advisable to check with your home insurer that you are covered for a nanny working in your home. In addition to that, and especially given the Ofsted requirements, a nanny should be insured to cover the eventuality of her causing injury to children in her care. See Appendix 2, pages 293–9.

Maternity and sick pay As employer, you are liable for both of these. Maternity rights in force at the time of writing give mothers-to-be a period of statutory leave of up to a year and it is automatically unfair to dismiss on grounds of pregnancy – but check the website for the current exact position. Most employers agree that it is good practice to pay your nanny even when she is sick. In the unlikely event that she is sick more often than a few days each year, withdrawing a discretionary payment might affect her performance in a positive way. At the end of the day, a nanny who is often ill will be replaced and will get a cautious reference, which should discourage her from taking days off with a runny nose. More details on maternity and sick pay can be found on the website.

Holiday pay and bank holidays Nannies, like all other employees, are entitled to four weeks' paid holiday per year, plus bank holidays. Normally a nanny will expect to be able to choose two of the weeks, with her employers choosing the other two. If the employer decides to take holiday over and above this, the nanny should still be paid. With big firms nowadays offering senior staff up to six weeks' annual leave, it is not uncommon for nannies to end up with a lot more holiday than the statutory minimum. Up-to-date information on holiday entitlement can be found on the website.

KEEPING YOUR NANNY HAPPY

As a general rule, happy nannies stay. As employers of nannies, we generally work, and most of us have been someone's employee. When we didn't feel we were being properly treated in a job, our performance was affected, and some of us left it for something better, didn't we? Now, of course, if the employee herself is the problem, it is unlikely that she will find something better elsewhere, but it is better to have the choice of whether to keep her or get rid of her.

A lot of research has been done into why nannies stay with employers and what most commonly causes them to leave a position. The results, though not groundbreaking, are worth bearing in mind.

What nannies say makes them happy and stay in a job are:

- liking my employer
- liking the children (interestingly in second place!)
- friendly, easygoing household
- employer showing appreciation
- respect for contractual hours and overtime pay

The most common causes of dissatisfaction are:

- employers' unreliability – at interview the nanny is told her hours are 8 a.m.–6.30 p.m., but in fact she ends up working till 7 p.m. most nights, without overtime pay
- employers interfering with the nanny's role – nannies traditionally prefer sole charge and things can get tricky when a parent is around. If you are around when your nanny is at work, sit down and discuss with her how you can best work together to avoid the conflict of authority, which causes children to misbehave and nannies to feel undermined
- not being paid on time – a standing order should deal with this one
- employers communicating with a nanny by scribbled notes rather than spoken word – sometimes leaving a note appears to be more efficient, but communications are much better conveyed and received orally, where you can

see the expression on the face of the person you are talking to

- employers not mentioning grumbles at the time, but bringing them up all together at a later date
- employers getting drunk/rowing in front of the nanny
- employers being indecisive or forgetful
- employers being over-demanding
- lack of praise – we all know how children respond better to praise than criticism: apply this to your nanny and you will be rewarded

However daunting that looks at first glance, it won't come as a surprise to many parents that they should communicate with respect and not get drunk in front of their employee. What is more surprising is that there is so much disrespectful and unprofessional behaviour among nanny employers.

It is impossible to predict how your relationship with your nanny will develop over time but there are a few basic rules you can follow to avoid problems.

Get everything in writing It is essential to spend time drafting your contract and to make sure that the nanny understands all the provisions, particularly relating to sick pay and holidays.

Tell it like it is Don't promise to be back punctually every night just to secure the right candidate for the job: you will not end up with someone who fits the reality.

Don't set your sights too high We all want our nanny to do a better job than we could, but if the nappy bin isn't empty at the end of the day occasionally, bear in mind that the baby's health and happiness is the real issue.

Set a review date Say two weeks into the job – when you can both sit down and talk through any issues that are bothering you. This is a chance to set a few extra rules that you hadn't thought of when drafting the contract, such as 'Please make a note of money you have spent each day'.

Make it a two-way thing When you raise an issue with the nanny, listen to her side of the story, and ask her how she thinks the issue could be resolved. This may give her more of a feeling of involvement and she will feel consulted, rather than just criticised.

Remember, she's new to it all However experienced or qualified your nanny may be, every job is a new household with new rules and new personalities. Her confidence will grow with time, as will yours in her.

Don't over-formalise your relationship Some high-flying career mothers can be over-systematic in managing their nanny. A formal appraisal may be a great idea in principle, but consider whether she might feel intimidated by the prospect . . .

DIFFICULTIES IN THE EMPLOYER–NANNY RELATIONSHIP

However carefully you have crossed the *t*s and dotted the *i*s in the contract, however diligently you praise, pay and respect your nanny, a change in circumstances, hers or yours, or even the actions or words of a third party over whom you have no control, may sow the seeds of discontent.

GENERAL GUIDANCE ON DEALING WITH NANNY PROBLEMS

We've looked at how to keep things going well in the employer–nanny relationship, but it's just as useful to have an emergency checklist of what and what not to do when things get difficult. In an employment relationship, especially one as personal as that of parent and nanny, it is vital to take a step back and a deep breath when a problem arises if the relationship is to have a chance of surviving and flourishing thereafter. Here are some golden rules for dealing with a nanny who is giving you problems.

- Don't ignore the warning signs of a nanny's discontent or of a decline in the standard of her work.
- Present a united front with your partner vis-à-vis the nanny.
- Don't gossip – the grapevine is all around you so try to stay in control of who knows what.
- Check the employment contract before taking any action relating to disciplinary issues or dismissal.
- Follow procedures, especially contractual disciplinary procedures, and keep the lines of communication open on all sides.
- Take great care if re-advertising the position, and communicate any confidentiality very clearly to any agency you are using. You don't want your nanny finding her job advertised on a website or to have an agency

speaking to her about interviews they are arranging with you.

➤ Take time off work if you need to, citing a family emergency. The care of your children is more important than a board meeting, and your employer is likely to be more understanding than you think.

SPECIFIC SITUATIONS THAT MAY CAUSE PROBLEMS IN THE RELATIONSHIP

A number of particular situations may arise during the course of a nanny's employment and result in friction in the parent–nanny relationship.

Health problems – yours and hers In the event that your nanny falls ill, your first task will be to find a temp to step in and take the reins. If the illness continues, you will need to think about statutory sick pay, because paying two nannies a full salary may not be a long-term solution. Your first port of call is the directgov website (see Resources, page 327) which has all the information you need on sick and maternity pay. Try to establish with your nanny, as tactfully as possible, the nature of the illness and, if possible, the prognosis, and help her to see things from your point of view in terms of replacing her while she is off.

If a working parent becomes ill, the nanny's job may change from sole to shared charge, or she may not be alone in the house with the children any more. Although this may seem an insignificant difference to you, a nanny sees things differently. Children are more likely to play up when they know a parent is around, and if she has chosen the position specifically because it is sole charge, you may need to reassure her about the change in circumstances. Your illness may also mean you need her to take on extra responsibilities or extend her working hours, and you should make sure she is happy with that. The alternative is to buy in other forms of help: ask your cleaner to do a few extra hours or persuade your family to shoulder some of the housekeeping burden.

Visitors If you have visitors staying at your house, especially with children, consider the effect of this on your nanny. It is not uncommon for parents to think nothing of giving their nanny extra children to look after in the holidays, and it may be that it doesn't involve much extra work for her but, as with any change in arrangements, make sure you check she is happy with the situation. If she feels she has been consulted she is much more likely to take on the extra responsibility with good grace. Offering to compensate her financially will usually soften the blow.

Role of the father and grandparents It is still the norm for mothers to organise childcare, and it is often the case that a nanny has little contact with the father. However, if an adult family member is installed in the house at the same time as a nanny, this can result in, at best, confusion over childcare roles, and at worst, the unconscious undermining of the paid carer by the family member. Clara, a qualified nanny in her thirties, remembers one job she had when the father was made redundant within a year of her joining the family:

I started working for the O'Neills when both parents worked full-time. As an experienced sole-charge nanny this was exactly what I was looking for – we had a handover period at the end of each day and I kept a diary showing what the children had been up to, what they'd eaten, who they'd played with. It all worked out brilliantly until the dad was made redundant and was suddenly around the house all the time, under my feet, interfering with the routine and giving me real problems keeping the children in order. I'm sure he had no idea of the trouble he was causing me – for him it was such a treat to be able to have more contact with his kids – and I didn't have the heart, or the words, to explain to him how I felt. He would appear just as I was dishing up lunch and Molly would start screaming in her high chair that she wanted Daddy, while Jack would jump up and try to start a wrestling match. Other times I might have an activity planned and Mike would announce he was taking the kids swimming or something. I felt kind of disabled by his presence. In the end I left because he started looking after the kids full-time, but it would never have worked long-term.

Other nannies report that in a family where the father takes responsibility for handovers, or is a lone parent, things seem to run more smoothly. Stuart tragically lost his wife Annabel shortly after the birth of his second daughter, and has always been the sole organiser of childcare in his home. His nanny, Shirley, has been with him for six years and says, 'It can be really different working for a man rather than a woman – sometimes mums can make you feel you're never as good as they are, you never quite measure up, but Stuart is a great dad and a great employer, and I know he's genuinely grateful for everything I do. It makes my job so much more rewarding as well.'

DIVORCE AND REMARRIAGE, DEATH AND NEW ARRIVALS

Anything involving changes in the family set-up can be a strain for the nanny as well as the parents and children.

New babies are expected and celebrated. Nannies don't usually expect a pay rise for the increased responsibility but recognition of that extra workload will always make them feel valued. It may detract from the temporary hurdle they experience in dealing with Mum being at home on maternity leave and a possible confusion in roles and duties as life readjusts.

With so many marriages ending in divorce these days, a nanny will probably not be surprised if her employers split up. She will be concerned about the longevity of her job prospects, though, so keep her informed about your plans, especially if a new baby is on the way or if you plan to move away altogether. Give her as much notice as possible. The danger of keeping things under wraps is that she may feel she has to jump before she is pushed, and you may lose a nanny you had planned to keep on, simply because she feels insecure.

Death is a subject you don't expect to read about in a book about nannies and nurseries. Yet in my years of running an agency I have met numerous nannies who have cared for dying children and the children of dying parents. I have found that tragedy can bring families and their nannies incredibly close – one mother described to me how her nanny was her lifeline during the short and tragic illness of her three-year-old boy.

Marta, an experienced Polish nanny, worked for a family in

which the mother was diagnosed with breast cancer while she was pregnant with the second baby. She died within two years and Tom, now seven, has no real memory of his mother. Marta is moved to tears even five years later when she talks about Clare's death, but felt challenged 'in a good way' by the change in her relationship with the children: 'I was the one person they were really close to who could talk to them about their mother without getting as emotional or upset as their other relatives would.'

TERMINATING THE NANNY–EMPLOYER RELATIONSHIP

When your nanny leaves, whether at her instigation or yours, and whether it's an amicable or a hostile departure, the knock-on effects can be rather similar to a divorce. As with any relationship, the longer you have been 'together', the harder it can be to separate. It's often especially hard on the children because they have been in the nanny's sole care and will have developed a bond of trust with her. They may feel confused, let down, even abandoned, so it's important to reassure them about the reasons for the nanny's departure so they don't assume the blame and feel guilty that somehow it's their fault.

Julia, a mother of three, had the same full-time nanny for four years before she moved on to a new job when the youngest child started school:

The children were heartbroken when Susie left. Our youngest had had her since he was a baby. After his brother and sister started school, Tom and Susie spent all their days together, and it was a bit of a shock to go from that level of intensity in a relationship to nothing at all – and it coincided with starting school, which, although providing a distraction for him, was also an important milestone he had to deal with without Susie to support him.

There is a lot you can do to make the transition easier. Here are a few tips.

- Be honest as far as you need to be with the children, but don't burden them with information inappropriate for their age.
- Listen to your children's worries about the nanny leaving and let them know their concerns have been heard and addressed.
- Let the children make a souvenir for your nanny to remember them by – a photo album or collage or just a handmade card.
- Reassure them, if possible, that the nanny will stay in contact – invite her to a child's birthday party or other happy occasion.
- Get the children involved in the search for a new nanny, so they feel they have a voice.
- On a practical level (and especially if the split has been acrimonious), inform nursery/school/activity groups that your children will be dropped off/collected by a new nanny.
- If the split has been acrimonious, you may need to tell your side of the story (as far as necessary and possible) to the nanny circle in which your children move, to teachers and other parents.

- Think carefully about having a 'break' between nannies because if the children get used to parents being around this can make it difficult to introduce a new carer at a later date.

Suzanne remembers:

We had the same nanny, Ellie, for seven years before she moved to Scotland to get married. She had been with us since our first child was six months old, and had become not just part of the family but an essential element that we just couldn't contemplate doing without. The weeks leading up to her departure were awful. I didn't want to tell the kids she was leaving until a short time before so they could carry on as normally as possible without worrying about it. We knew they would take it badly, and they did. We interviewed other nannies and one lovely one worked for us for a month before giving up because the kids were giving her such a hard time, comparing her to Ellie and making her feel inadequate. We then found another one who wasn't such an obvious fit with the family, but who had the personality to deal with whatever difficulties came up. She was very no-nonsense, and managed to distract the children from their preoccupation with Ellie by showing them that there was still fun to have, and that Ellie wasn't the only source of it! She realised how important it was to win their trust.

Nannies, although not the cheapest, are one of the most versatile and flexible forms of childcare. With the option of live-in or -out, longer hours than nurseries or childminders, and the convenience of having children of different ages cared for together at home, they offer the working parent the extra freedom that so many careers demand.

SUMMARY

If you are considering employing a nanny

- have you considered whether you need live-in or live-out?
- do you have the necessary accommodation for a live-in?
- is it within your budget (once you have calculated the tax and National Insurance applicable – see website)?
- will you be at home or at work? (Consider a mother's help if at home.)
- are your children all at school? (Consider an au pair.)

The most common reason for parents choosing not to employ a nanny but use other forms of childcare is, not surprisingly, cost. The next chapter deals with an increasingly popular and cost-effective alternative: nannysharing.

CHAPTER 5

Nannyshares

It's hardly surprising, with the total annual cost of hiring a full-time nanny between £33,000 and £40,000, that more and more families find sharing one, and substantially reducing the cost, an appealing option. Agency research shows that nearly 20 per cent of all nannies are currently in a share, and the demand for shares is on the increase.

A nannyshare, as the term is used in this chapter, occurs when two (or more) families employ the same nanny and when, for at least some of the time, she is looking after the children of both families simultaneously. This arrangement is distinct from the kind of sharing in which one family uses the nanny on, say, three days a week and the other on one or two days a week. In such cases, the families may never meet. It is also possible to employ a nanny with her own child, another form of share.

The main incentive for sharing a nanny is cost, but other factors motivate families to share – in particular the prospect of ready-made playmates for the children and a more sociable routine.

Theresa Byrne set up thenannysharers.co.uk: 'The costs involved in employing a nanny have traditionally put many people off. That's why nannysharing is becoming an increasingly popular choice . . . Families get all the benefits, but with the flexibility they need at a price they can afford.' A survey by thenannysharers showed that nearly three-quarters of parents agree: 'Seventy per cent thought nannysharing was the best childcare option . . . They believe it offers them quality and flexibility they wouldn't otherwise find.' Nannysharing might be the childcare solution for you if:

- you like the idea of a nanny but it's too expensive
- you have found 'the perfect family' to share with
- your children are older and your nanny has nothing to do while they are at school
- you are relaxed about having other children in your house
- you have one baby and feel he/she would benefit from company during the day, but would like some say in who that is
- you want a nanny but work from home and don't want your home to be the childcare setting

THE PRACTICALITIES OF NANNYSHARING

It seems like a marvellous idea at the NCT coffee morning to embark on your childcare project with your new best friend, whose baby was born two days after yours and who has experienced with you one of the most significant moments in your life. Most nannyshares start out in this way, with an agreement made in the back row of the baby-massage class or in the clinic waiting room. It's not uncommon for new mums returning to work to be intimidated by the institutional aspect of nurseries but equally put off by the high cost of a nanny. The nannyshare jumps out as the obvious answer and, indeed, is ideal in the case of two small babies.

However, there are a number of considerations you need to take into account before making the commitment. Friendships have broken down between children as well as parents because hasty arrangements have not been thought through properly. The most important piece of advice is to be honest and open with the share family as well as the nanny because trust and clarity are vital to keeping all the relationships healthy. Although the nanny may disappear off your radar if things go wrong, the other family will still be around and your children may become best friends with theirs.

A key point to note early on is that some families like to start sharing their nanny once their children begin nursery or school. It is important to remember that should you wish to change your nanny's terms of employment with a nannyshare arrangement you will need her agreement. It amounts to the termination of one contract of employment and the commencement of a new one and, strictly speaking, you should go through the legal motions to reflect this.

FINDING A FAMILY TO SHARE WITH

There are no ground rules about whom you should choose as your share family. Some parents advise sharing with a family you don't know so that you can be less emotional and more business-like about the arrangements. Other families go into shares with their best friends and experience no problems or complaints. You need to be practical about the choice you make in terms of location, ages of children and shared views on childcare, but don't ignore your gut instinct. If something isn't quite right, even if you can't put your finger on what it is, the chances are that it will loom larger at a later date.

If you haven't got a family in mind, but are keen to find one, you have a number of options.

- Contact a nanny agency in the usual way – most agencies are used to putting families in touch and may have several on their books who may be suitable. However, be aware that they are likely to charge both families the full fee if they find you a nanny to share. If you approach an agency with a ready-made share in mind, you will be able to split the agency fee between you.
- Look on the Internet – see Resources, page 324, for a list of websites that deal with nannysharing: the usual nanny-search websites will have plenty of families looking for a share.
- If you have already found a nanny, ask her to help you find a share family. The nanny network has considerable influence!
- Networking: as with all childcare searches, nothing beats the grapevine.

The big issues you need to address with your share partner are:

A shared childcare ethos Is the other mum a routines person or a born-again hippie? What works well in a friendship, in terms of opposites attracting, may not be such a success when it comes to raising babies. You can find out a lot about someone's approach to childcare just by observation.

- Watch her with the baby and her other children, if any. Listen to what she says about her values and views on childcare.
- Listen to her plans for the future. Is her baby destined to become a rocket scientist, to be fuelled from birth on a strict diet of imaginative play and verbal reasoning?
- How convinced is she about being a working mother? If she has doubts about going back to work, the family may pull out of the arrangement.
- Is she generous and relaxed or precious and protective? Most likely somewhere between the two, but it may happen that one parent in a share feels that her child is getting unequal treatment, so watch for a propensity to resentment.
- What are her views on activities? Some mothers like their children to benefit from every music class and toddler group going, so there may have to be compromise.

Timing and planning It sounds obvious but try to make sure that you know exactly when the other family needs the nanny to start, whether there will be a period when she is working for one family only, and whether the position is sole charge from the outset. Some nannies can be fussy about sole and shared charge (see Chapter 4, pages 104–6): if the other mother will be around the house for the first six months, this may limit your choice of candidates.

Find out whether the other family has any plans to move. If you take on a nanny who is specifically interested in sharing (which is likely to be for financial reasons), you may end up having to find a new family at short notice in order to keep her on. Try to agree between you as long a notice period as possible so that any impending move can be dealt with efficiently.

Are the other parents in the share planning to have more children, and if they do, will this affect the arrangements? If you have just one baby each at the start, it may be easy to incorporate an extra child in the future, but if there are already three in the share, a nanny might not be prepared to take on a fourth.

Feeding and sleeping If a nanny is looking after two babies at once, she will want to establish a consistent routine for both children, so you will need to agree on the two main aspects of any baby routine: feeding and sleeping. Discuss the question of diet (any allergies or special diet, views on organic food, processed food, jars, etc.) and naps (will the buggy or car seat do or is it to be the cot in a darkened room every time?) with your share partner. Be honest about what you want for your baby because it will be difficult to incorporate a change in your requirements at a later stage.

Discipline Shared views on discipline are important in a nannyshare. You can't have one child in a share sitting on the naughty step while the other is writing lines in the nursery. Discuss with your share partner what is acceptable to her in terms of discipline and boundaries. Any candidate you interview will want to be sure that you are all agreed on whether to use time out, the naughty step, or the positive-parenting plan. Little babies don't need much discipline, it's true, but as they get older they become a lot more mischievous and it's worth thinking about how to deal with the odd misdemeanour.

Treats and trips Your nanny will want to know how you feel about rewards and incentives for good behaviour, about television and DVDs, day trips to farms and play centres, and other adventures. Some parents like to reserve the best day trips for themselves as a family, and their noses are put out of joint when the nanny takes their offspring to Brighton beach and Alton Towers, leaving them with a more mundane itinerary for the weekend. How do you all feel about the nanny driving down motorways with your babies in the back seat? Some parents (myself included) would secretly prefer their nanny not to drive the children at all.

Share location At whose house will the share take place? If it's to be at yours, you may be able to leave your baby in bed in the morning and be spared a commute to the other house twice a day, but consider the wear and tear on your home, the possibility of damage to your property, your obligation to put up the appropriate safety equipment – stair gates and anti-slam devices on cupboards. Your fridge will house the week's food for all the children in the share, your sofas will be accommodating nanny-visitors, and your baby toys will be chewed and thrown not only by the other baby in the share but by all the visiting baby-friends. Ideally the share should take place at the house of the family that is most relaxed about it, but many parents like to alternate with one week at each house so that both get a fair share of the damage.

If you intend that the nanny will pick up one baby from one house and transport him to the second house, consider the timing and logistics for this from the nanny's point of view, including traffic, parking and the added time on her working day.

Whatever you decide, make sure that the home at which the share is to take place has all the necessary toys and equipment, and remember that you will have to share the cost of a double buggy and possibly a second high-chair. If your child is to be based away from home, make sure you take his favourite toys with him so that he feels comfortable, and leave a spare set of clothes at the house for emergencies.

Holidays One major stumbling block for sharers is working out the nanny's annual leave. In a traditional nanny set-up, the nanny will choose half of the holiday period and the employer the other half. Often, an employer will need to take all her leave in the school holidays and the nanny will not, so the nanny ends up getting extra paid holiday and parents have to bring in temps to cover her term-time absence. In a share, the 50/50 split means that each family will only be able to nominate one week in a year. An alternative would be to agree on a three-way split, but nannies are not generally keen to relinquish their 50 per cent, the main reason being the huge increase in travel costs during school holidays.

Sickness Consider what will happen when one of the children in the share is sick. The main issue is passing infection to the other child. A runny nose is hardly a serious problem but with a severe tummy bug, or worse, you may want to keep your baby at home. Then, when the boot is on the other foot, you will be in a good position to suggest the other family does the same. If your child gets chicken pox or head lice, you should warn your share family as soon as possible.

If your nanny is sick, are you able to pay a temp between you, or will your share partner expect you to do without?

If you are sick and the share takes place at your home, is your share partner prepared to have the nanny work at her house that day?

FINDING THE RIGHT NANNY

Finding a nanny for a share is just like finding any other nanny, except that she needs to be approved not only by your partner and children but by the other family. Ideally you would all meet potential candidates together, but in practice this can be intimidating for a nanny, so it is more common for one family to meet her first and involve the other if they feel she has potential. If both families agree a shortlist from the CVs supplied, and each family does a first interview with half of the candidates chosen, this may speed up the process.

Hopefully your candidate will have previous experience of a share or, in the case of two babies, have worked with twins. Nursery nurses make good candidates as they are likely to have had responsibility for three babies at once in the nursery setting.

INTERVIEWING YOUR NANNY

When interviewing a nanny for a share, you will ask roughly the same questions as you would in a normal nanny interview, with some adaptation to the share circumstances. Here is a basic list.

1. What does she like most about being a nanny?
2. Are there any aspects of sharing she is apprehensive about?
3. What experience of shares or twins does she have?
4. How organised is she? (Managing two employers requires efficiency and resilience.)
5. How did she get on with the children in her last job?
6. How did she get on with the parents in previous jobs?
7. How does she feel about having two sets of employers? Can she foresee any difficulties?
8. Has anything annoyed her or upset her about her employers in previous jobs?
9. What activities would she do with children aged X and Y?
10. What sort of meals would she prepare for them?
11. Does she have a current first-aid certificate? If not can she deal with/has she ever dealt with a first-aid emergency?
12. What is she getting paid in her current job?
13. What are her salary expectations for a share?
14. Does her employer know she is looking for work?
15. Why is her current job ending?
16. What are her long-term plans and how long does she want a job for?

Interviewing is a two-way process. Give her the chance to ask you questions and make sure you tell her:

- all about your children – their likes and dislikes, their personalities, funny ways, and how they currently get on with the other children in the proposed share
- your views on discipline – would she feel happy following the procedures advocated by you and your share partner?
- your and your share partner's joint and agreed views on television, videos, sweets and other treats
- your requirements regarding activities – if it is important that your child can continue to attend a particular playgroup, for example, can she handle any complications caused by having two families with different organised activities?
- your requirements regarding any additional duties, such as washing and ironing, occasional grocery shopping, running errands to the dry-cleaner, the post office, etc. Think what needs doing in each house, if the share is divided between the two
- your work schedules, the exact hours she will be needed, any babysitting or holiday work, whether you will be at home for any of the time she is working – and whether she may care for the children in your share partner's house if you are at home
- the exact salary – whether it's a daily or hourly rate, whether gross or net
- whether you will pay for her petrol/parking permit/car insurance, and which family's car she will use
- any perks, like gym membership, extra holiday, etc.
- with holiday in particular, discuss any holidays you or she may already have planned, and your ongoing

requirements regarding taking holiday within school holidays. Is she happy with the standard procedure of employers choosing half of the holiday dates and the nanny choosing the other half?

- how long you will need a nanny for and whether the post is likely to stop being a share at some point in the future, perhaps if you both have more children

Agree with your share partner who will check the references; there is no harm in duplicating checks, if you feel it necessary. It is vital that both families go into the share with full confidence in the nanny.

FINANCE AND CONTRACTUAL ISSUES

Contracts, tax and NICs You will need a written contract of employment with your nanny, just as you would if it was not a share. A single contract should suffice, with you and your share partner together referred to as the employer. Separate contracts with each family are needed when the nanny works some days for one family and the rest for the other.

As with any nanny, you should specify a gross salary in the contract to protect you from any unforeseen increases in tax liability due to her taking on other work, or due to any underpayment from previous employment. For the latest advice on tax and NIC issues relating to shares, and details of payroll companies who can help you sort out the tax side, see Appendix 2, pages 293–9, and the website.

Sharing the cost of the nanny In a straightforward situation with two babies in a full-time share with the same hours, a 50/50 split on costs is logical. However, you may have to adjust the split if:

- the nanny is living in with one of the families
- the nanny is benefiting from a car or other perks from one family
- the nanny is working longer hours or babysitting for one family
- one family has more children than the other

Exactly how you apportion the costs will depend on the individual situation, but openness and honesty from the outset will minimise the chance of resentment building up later.

Nannyshare salaries As a general rule of thumb, a full-time nanny of average experience and qualifications working for just one family in the London area can expect to earn (net to them) around £450–550 per week. In a share, they can reasonably expect to be paid up to 20 per cent more per day. This is a very general guideline, and salaries vary considerably depending on location, and the age, experience and qualifications of the nanny.

Other expenses Any nanny is going to incur daily expenses as part of her job, for petrol, entrance fees, food and other necessities. Discuss with your share partner the use of a car (if relevant) and how you will divide the cost of motor insurance, and any additional charges relating to household insurance.

Remember to factor in the cost of essential equipment, like double buggies and high-chairs.

PROS AND CONS OF SHARING A NANNY

The benefits of sharing a nanny include:

- sociable for children, and you choose their playmates (unlike at nursery or with a childminder)
- the cost – although not halved, it is substantially reduced
- if the location is shared or elsewhere, there is less wear and tear on your home
- all the usual benefits of a nanny (see page 76)

The disadvantages include:

- complications over holiday requirements with differing schedules
- disagreements possible over routines, discipline, nanny's role
- household insurance policy may not cover accidental injury the other child suffers – consult insurers
- one family may pull out
- need to evaluate the safety and childproofing of the host home (Is it childproofed to the right level to cover all relevant age groups? Is there a pond or swimming-pool?)
- need to allocate and record cost of nappies and other supplies

- disagreements that one family has with the nanny may overflow to the other

Katie shared a nanny with another family when she had her first baby:

> *I first started using childcare when William was seven months old. We did a nannyshare with another family who had a daughter six months older than William. I found the nannyshare on a website and was incredibly lucky in that the family we shared with was looking for a new family – the one they were sharing with was moving away. This meant they had everything in place – a fantastic nanny they had been using for the last eight months, two high-chairs, two cots, a double buggy, etc. Because the other family were so fond of the nanny and I liked her straight away, and because they had already worked with her for eight months, I was happy and confident with the set-up. If I hadn't found this, I would have struggled to decide what to do.*
>
> *The main concern I had was that the share was at the other family's home, and they had established a good relationship already with the nanny. I didn't want the other child to have preferential treatment or for the nanny to be occupied doing chores for the other family rather than looking after the children. These concerns were allayed by time and seeing how happy William was. I had addressed the concerns with the other family and the nanny, and was assured that it was all very equal but only time and seeing for myself reassured me that this really was the case.*
>
> *I think I was really lucky with my first experience of*

childcare – the nannyshare worked out brilliantly and only came to an end when I and the other mother had another baby at the same time. The nanny, Rebecca, has now returned home to New Zealand so the experience came to a natural end. William absolutely adores Isabella – the girl he shared Rebecca with – and learnt loads from her as she was that little bit older.

NANNIES WITH OWN CHILDREN

Some nannies come to work with their own babies or toddlers, or bring a school-age child to work after school hours and during the holidays – nannying is one of the few careers where bringing your offspring to work is not just possible but in some cases welcomed by an employer. An extra child in the house will be company for yours, yet you won't be dealing with another employer family, which may make things easier. The cost will be less than that of a nanny without a child, but more than you would pay in a standard nannyshare when the nanny is effectively being compensated for having two employers.

Many parents are understandably concerned about where their child will come in the pecking order – surely the nanny's child comes first? Amazingly, most nannies won't hesitate to reassure you that your own child will come first every time, and theirs will fit in with your chosen routine. The arrangement can work brilliantly, but if things do go sour, bear in mind that your child will lose a friend as well as a nanny.

A nanny with her own child may be the right option for you if:

- you want your child to have the company of other children
- you want your childcare to be home-based
- you are uncertain about setting up a childcare arrangement with another family
- you are reassured by the idea of a nanny who is herself a mother
- you have fewer than three children
- you meet a brilliant nanny and are prepared to take her on any terms

PROS

- Cost – lower than a nanny all to yourself.
- Home-based childcare so less settling in.
- Reassuring to have a nanny who is herself a mother.
- No other share family to deal with.
- You can choose half of the annual holiday dates, rather than a quarter as in a normal share.
- Nanny is less likely to take a day off sick as she will have her own child with her and may find it easier to cope with a minor illness if her child has a playmate.

CONS

- Nanny may not come to work if her *child* is sick.
- More expensive than a standard share, nursery or childminder.
- You may have to childproof your house to a level relevant to her child and not just yours.

- Your house may be cluttered with her child's paraphernalia, which your child is too young or too old for.
- No option for this kind of share being hosted in another house.
- A nanny with one child is likely to want another at some point, and this may disrupt your arrangement.

Marian, a part-time solicitor, was one of those who had assumed the nanny's child would take priority:

> *I was drawn originally to the idea of nannysharing because of the financial aspect, but I couldn't find the right family at short notice and an agency I spoke to suggested using a nanny with her own child. At first this seemed a strange idea – I couldn't get away with taking my baby to work so how was it that nannies were allowed to? Persuaded by the agent on the phone, I set up an interview and was very pleasantly surprised. Michelle brought her year-old daughter with her and my six-month-old Harry was immediately fascinated by his new playmate. Having a child slightly older than mine to bring him on development-wise was definitely an advantage, and having a nanny who was a mother was even more confidence-inspiring. My husband and I were concerned about priorities – surely her own child would come first as a matter of instinct? Michelle reassured us that Harry's needs would take first priority and my fears were allayed. We hired Michelle and the arrangement continued until I left my job two years later, and I am sure that Harry really benefited from it the whole way through. As far as priorities were concerned, it was always Harry's routine that prevailed, and when it came to naps, meals and activities, I felt comfortable and*

confident knowing that my requirements were all being met. I would recommend nanny with own child to anyone.

If there were any bad points, it would probably be the same as with any share – the wear and tear on your house, the need to consider the developmental stage of the other child or children in terms of stair gates and cupboard locks, etc. But, of course, the big plus in using a nanny with a child is you have the financial benefit without the headache of the inter-share politics. Your nanny is your own and doesn't have conflicting commitments to another employer. You also avoid the holiday problem, as it works just like in a straightforward nanny situation.

Here is my own experience of nannysharing:

I am a very keen advocate of nannies with own children. I have employed three different nannies who brought their offspring to work, first when I had one child, then when I had three. The nanny I employed at that point had her own two-year-old and was seven months pregnant with her second. My children were two, four and six, so you can imagine what a challenge that would be for anyone! Katie was an absolute superstar. As well as being incredibly professional, she was clearly really interested in children, their development and education, and in having fun with them. When I met her I was interviewing her through my agency, but as soon as she walked through the door I decided to employ her myself, however many other children she might have.

Through being a mother she knew the tried and tested ways of dealing with tantrums and the terrible twos, she was perfectly used to supervising some Play-Doh or fingerpainting with one eye on the pasta cooking on the stove. To cap it all, she was a trained chef and ran a catering business on the side, so my children ate like royalty, and found baked beans on toast at the weekends a bit of a let-down.

Katie had to leave to have her own baby, and after that wanted to work part-time, or I would definitely have had her back. But my next nanny (and, remember, I have the choice of hundreds coming through the books every year) was another I chose specifically because she was a mother herself. Again, Cara had this extra layer of common sense and responsibility that comes with being a parent, she was perfectly capable of working to my routine, and getting her son to fit in with it, and she had a certain confidence when it came to discipline and authority that you just can't find in a textbook or get from a course. Interestingly Cara left me for a full-time job with a family of four – which just goes to show what she was capable of and how when a parent meets a great nanny, the fact she may have her own child is of very little consequence.

SUMMARY

Before deciding on nannysharing, have you considered:

- your reasons for choosing a share over your own nanny or other childcare?
- the suitability of the other family, particularly in terms of ethos, location and practical requirements?
- the ages, nature and general suitability of the other children in the share?
- whether the nanny in question has the right level of experience for a share?

Sharing a nanny works wonderfully for some families and some nannies enjoy the variety and the challenge of multiple responsibilities. Parents appreciate having home-based care at a lower cost, and most discover that the benefits of a successful share are well worth the complications of finding, arranging and maintaining it.

CHAPTER 6

Au Pairs and Babysitters

The reason that au pairs and babysitters are dealt with together in this chapter is because both offer part-time childcare, and babysitting is an element of the au-pair job description.

AU PAIRS

An au pair is an overseas visitor, a single person aged between 17 and 27 who comes on a cultural-exchange programme to learn another language and help in a family home. She (or he) will live in your house as part of your family and will need their own bedroom. An au pair is normally expected to work 25 hours a week and must have time off to attend language classes. She should not be left in sole charge of children under the age of two. Au-pair placements are for a maximum of two years. You will not usually meet your au pair before she starts work because they are recruited from within the country of origin. Typically an au pair will be from an educated, middle-class European family and her parents will want her to spend a year abroad, immersing herself in a foreign culture for her educational advancement.

Some nannies come to the UK from overseas with CVs that mention 'au-pair work' and their perception of the definition may be rather different. In South Africa for example the term 'au pair' is used to describe a live-out after-school carer; most commonly these will be students working part-time after college and in the holidays. So when you hear the words 'au pair' check that it means what you think it means!

TYPES OF AU PAIR

Just as there are different definitions of an au pair, so the market has created numerous different 'types' to respond to social demand, but essentially there are three main types of au pair recognised in the UK.

- *Au pair*: works up to 25 hours per week plus babysitting.
- *Au pair plus*: works up to 35 hours per week plus babysitting (although the European guidelines actually specify 30 hours as the absolute maximum on a cultural-exchange programme).
- *Mother's help*: a definition used by some agencies to describe a live-in helper (from abroad) who earns substantially less than a nanny but works a longer day and earns more than an au pair.

An au pair may be the childcare solution for you if:

- cost is an issue and nannies are too expensive an option
- your children are over three
- you have a spare room in the house
- you are a warm and welcoming family
- you have time to train and help someone learn to do the job to your liking
- you wish to create a better work–life balance in your family
- you need an extra pair of hands around the house
- your children could benefit from sharing their talent for sport, art or music with another young person
- you would like more quality time with your children
- you want to take the stress out of the school run, have more sleep, or just spend more quality time with your partner
- you work shifts or weekends
- you would like to give a young person a chance to improve their language skills and learn about life in Britain
- you would like your children to learn a few words of another language along the way
- you care for an elderly relative in your home and would like some help and companionship for them
- you have pets and need some help with their care or dog walking

DUTIES

An au pair's exact duties will vary from family to family depending on the number and ages of children and whether or not both parents work. In essence, their tasks will include light housework, cleaning, washing up, ironing, helping at mealtimes, with school runs, and generally with the children. Typically, your au pair will get the children ready for school in the morning, pick them up in the afternoon, cook their tea, help with homework or play until you come home, or until she is off duty. Some au pairs will show particular aptitude for particular chores: Sally Marshall found her male au pair was excellent at ironing but hopeless at cooking so they made a deal: 'Once I found out how great he was at ironing I asked him (very politely, of course) whether he would take over that task from the cleaner so she could concentrate on the cleaning. I absolved him completely from cooking duties, which was great for him, and for the children, who are very fussy eaters and did nothing but complain about his culinary efforts!'

When discussing duties with your au pair, be sure to demonstrate what is required, and share the chores initially so you can give helpful advice without it sounding like a telling-off. Most au pairs will be eager to please and will appreciate your help initially, particularly given language and cultural barriers. The Philips family have had a series of au pairs and have noticed that the more hands-on induction they are given, the better the job they do: 'We were naïve with our first au pair, pointing out where the Hoover was but not explaining about the different nozzles and how to empty the bag. When the bag exploded I had to bite my tongue and remember the poor girl was much more upset than I was. Now I take the time to go through everything in minute detail, and not all of it in one go. It can take a week or so before they know what they're doing, and that's not bad considering it's often completely and utterly alien to them at first!'

The British Au Pair Agencies Association (BAPAA) has the following recommendations relating to au pair duties:

List of housework duties accepted as light housework under the au pair programme:

- washing dishes, including loading and unloading dishwasher
- preparing simple meals for children
- keeping kitchen tidy and clean, including sweeping and mopping floors
- loading and unloading washing-machine
- ironing for children
- putting washed clothes away
- vacuuming
- dusting
- making and changing children's beds
- cleaning children's bathroom
- everything to do with keeping their own room/bathroom clean and tidy
- light shopping (not all the household shopping)
- walking and feeding pets
- emptying bins

List of duties considered unsuitable for an au pair:

- gardening
- window-cleaning

- spring-cleaning
- cleaning the oven, other than simple wiping out
- washing carpets
- washing the car
- weekly shopping
- pet training
- clearing up after untrained pets
- making parents' bed*
- ironing for parents*
- cleaning parents' en-suite bathroom*
- polishing silver and brassware*
- cooking the family meal, unless the au pair enjoys cooking and has chosen to do this for the family

*These tasks may be included where there is less childcare and the children are out of the house for most of the day.

Au pairs should not be required to do housework, such as ironing, when looking after children of primary-school age or toddlers.

DIFFERENCES BETWEEN AN AU PAIR AND A LIVE-IN NANNY

Au pair	Nanny
Not available for interview	Available for interview
Around £70 per week	Around £300 per week, live-in
Not likely to be qualified	Should be either qualified or have appropriate experience

Suitable for over-twos only	Suitable for all ages of children
Limited to 25–35 hours per week	Can work a 60-hour week
Babysitting two nights a week included	Babysitting not included
Eats with the family, to be included as one of the family	Less pressure to include her as one of the family
Aged 17–27	Any age
Placement limited to two years	No limit on placement
Limited amount of light housework included	Housework not included unless specifically agreed
Non-native English	May be native English

ACCOMMODATION

It may seem obvious but an au pair is entitled to her own bedroom (not shared with any children). It should be free of any family possessions (including children's clothing stored in the cupboards or drawers) to allow complete privacy. The room should be of reasonable size, with natural light, a desk or small table and chair, to allow the au pair to study in her free time. If there is no desk in the room, the au pair must be allowed to use another table or desk in the house (dining room, family office, etc.)

NATIONALITY AND VISAS

Au pairs may come from anywhere in Europe under the au pair programme. The visa situation for au pairs changes regularly: the latest information will be available to view on the Home Office website (see Resources, page 320). Make sure you are informed of the current visa restrictions that may apply. There are many candidates on au-pair websites from countries where there is no au-pair visa for Britain; inviting them into your household with a potentially inappropriate visa would make their stay illegal.

If you employ an au pair from the European Economic Area (EEA) there are a number of practical advantages:

- no restrictions on duration, age and working hours, giving you the utmost flexibility for your au-pair requirement
- no visa needed – if you need someone quickly, a visa application may cause delay
- EEA driving licences can be used in Britain for up to 12 months
- if you travel frequently on short breaks or long-haul, an au pair from another EEA country can go with you without obtaining a visa
- many local colleges offer part-funded language courses provided by the council, like ESOL courses, but they are usually restricted to European nationals
- it is easier and more affordable for EEA au pairs to go home for a break

All au pairs must have a valid passport and, if they require an au-pair visa, must have a letter of invitation from the host family to obtain one.

STUDYING

The primary purpose of an au-pair placement in the UK is to allow single people to improve their English-language skills and to experience English culture and life by living with an English-speaking family. Families must respect this, and ensure that the au pair's duties do not interfere with studying commitments.

Normally au pairs want to study at a local college for a qualification. Your au pair will need to enrol in person as soon as she can after arriving. She will have to pay the fees in advance and will normally be tested to decide which class is best suited to her level of English. Some families provide assistance with the fees – it may be difficult for an au pair to pay in advance on arrival – but there is no obligation to do so. When you have engaged an au pair, find out about English courses in your area and plan for her to arrive around the enrolment date.

CARS AND DRIVING

If you require a driver, and your au pair is not from an EEA member state, make sure she obtains an International Driving Licence before she leaves home. Needless to say, you should assess the driving ability of your au pair before letting her drive on her own. Some families pay for a few driving lessons in their car as practice for the au pair and as a means of assessing her ability. If your au pair is to drive your car, be clear about any restrictions on its use.

- Can she use it in her free time or is it only for use when she is working for the family?

- Does she provide receipts or will you give her a weekly allowance for petrol?
- Is she allowed to give lifts to friends?
- Is she responsible for cleaning it? (This is not a suitable duty for au pairs according to BAPAA guidelines.)

Nearly half of the au pairs placed by agencies are drivers. In Western Europe the driving test is considered tough, and traffic levels are similar to those in the UK so most au pairs who drive will adapt quickly to driving over here. Eastern European (and Turkish) au pairs may need extra lessons in the UK to become satisfactorily competent.

FREE TIME

All au pairs are entitled to two free days each week. This should usually be two 24-hour periods and only cancelled in an emergency. All BAPAA agencies run a monthly excursion programme for au pairs during their stay in the UK, which takes the pressure off a busy family at weekends! BAPAA also offers discounted paediatric first-aid courses.

Holiday entitlement

An au pair is entitled to a minimum two weeks' paid holiday per year; one week for every six-month stay. If the placement is for a shorter time, holiday is calculated pro rata. The au pair should not be forced to take holiday to coincide with the family holiday.

Social life

Not surprisingly, most au pairs are keen to have some sort of social contact during their stay with you, but you probably won't be keen on having a houseful of strange teenagers raiding your fridge and playing loud music. In fact, most au pairs are happy to socialise outside the home but it's a good idea to have clear rules in place. An au pair should ask her host if she may bring friends back to the house and should not expect to do so without permission. Most employers of au pairs have only positive things to say about this side of things, but it's worth taking note of a story that paints a slightly different picture. Christine's first au pair was from Slovakia:

> *It was her first visit to England and she was one of those very extrovert girls, very pretty and lovely and sociable, and went out a lot. Lots of our friends had au pairs who never went out at first and moped around all homesick, so we thought we were quite lucky. Then she found a boyfriend and started being out even more, occasionally all night, and was late back (and very hung-over so not much use) a couple of mornings when we needed her to do the school run. By then it was almost too late to introduce new rules – it felt as if we had let things go too far, and it was very awkward sitting her down and trying to rein her in. If you're not a confrontational person this can be a real problem, so I would advise anyone to be quite strict about social life. I also think we are like proxy parents and have a responsibility to the girl's parents to keep her in line somehow! It is important to start as you mean to go on – it's always easier to give more freedom once you know the maturity level of your au pair and can trust her to go out and return safe and sound, happy to do breakfast duties and the school run the next day.*

QUALIFICATIONS

Au pairs are unlikely to be qualified in childcare and some have little or no experience of it. A mother's help au pair should have a wider range of childcare experience. It is advisable for any au pair to be first-aid trained, and a list of courses can be found in the Resources section, page 328, and on the website. Some agencies recommend courses for au pairs. Smart Au Pairs, based in Kent but covering the whole of the UK, offers parents the opportunity to enrol their au pairs on an Apprenticeship in Children's Care Learning and Development course which includes:

- NVQ Level 2 in Children's Care Learning and Development
- BTEC Level 2 in Children's Care Learning and Development
- Key Skills in Communication (English language) and Application of Numbers Level 1
- 12-hour paediatric first-aid course
- general advice on employment rights and responsibilities

The benefits to the au pair are:

- a recognised qualification in childcare
- a chance to network with other students during monthly visit to training centre
- home visits from training assessor
- the opportunity to earn and learn
- improved employability in UK and Europe
- no college to attend except monthly tutorials
- professional support from training company throughout

The benefits to the family are:

- an au pair with long-term commitment
- an au pair with a real interest in childcare
- a structured development programme to enhance the care received by the child(ren) as the au pair is learning
- visits from professional assessor to monitor progress
- no need for the au pair to attend college, just one monthly tutorial on a Saturday

COSTS

The salary you pay your au pair will depend on the type of au pair she is and the hours she works:

Au pair (25–30 hours per week)
- recommended pay from £70
- includes five hours per day, five days per week and two to three evenings' babysitting per week
- no sole care for children under two

Au pair plus (30–35 hours per week)
- recommended pay £85
- includes six hours per day, five days per week and two to three evenings' babysitting per week
- no sole care for children under two

Mother's help (35+ hours per week)*
- weekly pay from £120
- includes up to 10 hours per day, five days per week and two to three evenings' babysitting per week

- more responsibility, younger children and/or longer hours

*The mother's help is not included in the au-pair cultural-exchange scheme. Candidates are willing and able to take on higher levels of responsibility and their visa status permits it. This mother's help is distinct from the one described in Chapter 2 in that she lives in rather than out.

If an au pair works longer hours in the school holidays, pay should be increased accordingly.

When weighing up the costs of an au pair, remember there may be a few hidden extras over and above board and lodging, such as:

- cost of petrol from use of car in her spare time
- taking your au pair on holiday with you
- Internet access
- mobile phone
- membership of gym or sports club
- payment towards English classes, first-aid qualification, travel on public transport
- payment (exceptional) of a flight home after agreed period of successful performance

You may also want to think about offering a higher salary to your au pair to reflect:

- her previous childcare experience
- the level of responsibility she will be required to take
- the number of children she will be looking after

- the age of the children
- how much sole charge she will have
- whether she is a driver
- the level of her education and spoken English

Agency fees vary widely but are generally considerably lower than nanny-agency fees and are based on the length of time the au pair will be with you.

PROS

The main advantages of an au pair over other forms of childcare are that:

- she can help with light housework
- she is a 'built-in' babysitter, although you must agree terms and conditions for this beforehand
- she can help your child understand another culture/language
- she may be interested in music or sport and inspire your children
- she may become a close friend to you and the children
- good company if you are a lone parent

CONS

The main disadvantages of an au pair over other forms of childcare are that:

- she is unlikely to be qualified
- she is unlikely to have much childcare experience on arrival

- you will have no opportunity to meet her in person if you recruit from overseas via an agency
- she cannot provide full-time, sole-charge childcare
- you may find it hard having someone else living in your house
- cooking skills usually leave something to be desired
- she may not know how to cope when the going gets tough
- it is your responsibility to make sure she knows the basics of childcare and first aid, and has suitable back-up in case of emergency
- there may be language or communication difficulties
- you'll almost certainly need to provide emotional support for a homesick au pair – think of yourself at 18!

HEALTH AND INSURANCE

Au pairs from the EEA can receive medical treatment in the UK under reciprocal healthcare agreements. Au pairs from other countries should confirm with the embassy prior to their departure for the UK the reciprocal healthcare agreement available, but will be entitled to receive emergency treatment from GPs or hospitals (they may be charged a fee in some situations). An au pair should register with the family doctor and dentist as a temporary patient on her arrival.

All au pairs should be covered by the household insurance policy although you should consider arranging additional insurance to cover emergencies – check your policy.

Most agencies will advise au pairs to have adequate personal and medical insurance prior to their departure from their home country.

TRAVEL

The au pair is expected to pay the cost of her return travel to and from the UK. As a host family you will be expected to meet your au pair at her point of arrival. In some circumstances, agencies can arrange onward travel but will usually ask families to reimburse their au pair with the cost.

WHERE TO FIND AN AU PAIR

DIY route: magazines, newspapers, libraries, websites

Many home helpers advertise in magazines, newspapers, on the Internet or, if they are looking to change family once they are here, on library and community notice-boards. You can place your own advert in any of these places, but if you take the DIY route, remember to check references and speak to any previous employers directly, rather than relying on written recommendations. If it takes someone five minutes to decide that they want to be au pair, it may also take them five minutes to decide it's not for them, and this may be when you have a sick child and an important meeting ahead of you!

Grapevine

Nothing beats a personal recommendation so ask other parents if they know of any au pairs looking for a new 'home' or if they can recommend a good agency. Perhaps your neighbour's au pair has a friend looking for work, but be aware that the friend of a good au pair may not be a good au pair herself.

Agencies

The safest way to look for an au pair is by using an au pair agency. The agency doesn't need to be local to you (unlike a nanny agency) as most will place au pairs anywhere in the country. Look online for agencies that are members of either the British Au Pair Agencies Association (BAPAA) or the Recruitment and Employment Confederation (REC): such agencies will have had to comply with strict codes of conduct that may be viewed on their websites. For example, BAPAA member organisations must:

- offer the highest standard of service and customer care
- be financially sound
- have strict screening processes in place
- offer ongoing personal care for the au pair during his or her stay

Agency procedures

A list of agencies that are members of the BAPAA is set out on pages 313–20. If you use the Internet, be prepared to do your homework to ensure that the candidate is vetted, well informed about the programme and able to stay in Britain legally as an au pair. Some nanny agencies deal with au pairs, but the procedure for sourcing and placing them is different from the nanny process, so most will specialise in one area or the other. Agency fees are lower for au pairs than they are for nannies, but you may be required to pay a deposit on registration, which is usually refundable against any placement fee.

Agencies recruit au pairs from their country of origin. Usually they work in partnership with an agency in that country, which interviews and vets all candidates. The partner agencies can vary in standard and quality so it's worth making some enquiries of the UK agency as to their partner's recruitment procedures.

The usual procedure for recruiting an au pair is to register online or by phone with the agency, which will then contact you to discuss your requirements and take a deposit if applicable. The agency will want as much information as possible from you about your family and what you are looking for so that they can find you the best possible match. As well as providing a family photo showing you all at your best and smiliest (because au pairs say this is the first thing they look at) make sure you tell them:

- your expectations of the role that the au pair will play in your family
- the accommodation you will provide
- whether your children have a special skill, passion or talent – you may be looking for the au pair to have an interest or a skill in this area too
- all the positive reasons for joining your family, which may include the distance to the nearest station, language school or the centre of town, use of the car in their spare time, learning to play tennis/ride a horse/sail a yacht

Au pairs are not generally accomplished housekeepers and cooks on their arrival so it's as well to be realistic about your expectations, and also to be prepared to pay more for a candidate if they have childcare experience, language and cooking skills or a driving licence. If any of these elements is important to you, make clear that the salary will reflect this.

The agency should then produce a shortlist of candidates, usually viewable online, each with her own information pack, including:

- 'Dear Family' letter telling you about herself, her home and her own family
- notes from the partner-agency interview
- photo
- references
- medical certificate
- police check

You then contact the ones you want to interview. The agency should be able to advise you on questions to ask. Interviews take place over the phone, or using Skype, and most agencies recommend a webcam for a more personal experience.

ONCE YOUR AU PAIR ARRIVES . . .

The best way to start planning for your au pair's arrival is to imagine yourself at her age and imagine how you might have felt to be going to a foreign country, perhaps for the first time, leaving your own family to live with people you have never met. This is a difficult and stressful time for a young person, however calm she may seem on the surface.

Prepare her room as you would like to find it. She will need a wardrobe and a desk, with curtains or blinds at the window. If you include a TV and DVD player, you will not only give her the opportunity to improve her English but will gain some privacy in the evenings if she can entertain herself in her room.

Pictures on the walls, flowers in a vase, a bowl of fruit are all little luxuries that will make her feel special, but only start as you mean to go on or you will find yourself turning into a chambermaid and folding her sheet down every night and scattering rose petals over the bed . . .

An au pair is intended to be a member of your family, so make her feel welcome – and make sure the rest of the family does too. It can be difficult to persuade children to be friendly to a stranger in the house, but it will help if you tell them how important it is to make the new arrival feel at home. Why not ask the children to help prepare the room?

Although the au pair will book and pay for her flight to the UK, you should meet her at the airport. Bear in mind that she may have been nervous and unable to sleep much the night before, and try to make her arrival in your home calm and easy. Supper together on her first night should be simple and straightforward, so you can concentrate on getting to know each other rather than cooking and washing up.

The next day is the best time to get down to showing her round and explaining the household routine and her role. One seasoned au-pair employer advises, 'You have to get the timing right with this – too soon and you might overwhelm her, but wait too long and she may well get too used to the freedom and forget she has a job to do!' Ideally give her a timetable to refer to and a list of chores that will be her responsibility *after* you have shown her around. She is much more likely to digest her written job description if she has seen where you keep the Hoover and how to work the dishwasher.

It's easy to forget that your au pair's primary reason for being in your home is to learn English, and she will be anxious to know when and how to get to her place of study: when you show her around the area where you live, start with that. Once she knows where she has got to be and when, she will be relaxed enough to take in the rest of the information. Other places you should make her aware of are your local shops, doctor's surgery, school, church and leisure facilities. She will also need to know how local transport works, where the nearest station and bus stop are and how to get around. Remember, you want her days off to be days off – however much you wish her to be part of your family, you will need some time on your own at weekends.

An au pair from the EEA is relatively simple to administer, but au pairs from countries outside the EEA will need to register with the local police station within seven days of arrival. She will need her passport, two passport-sized photographs, and she is personally responsible for any fee payable.

ESTABLISHING A GOOD RELATIONSHIP WITH YOUR AU PAIR

Keeping your relationship with your au pair healthy and happy is a job in itself. Unlike a live-in nanny, who is likely to disappear discreetly at appropriate moments, your au pair knows she is supposed to be part of your family and will expect to be included in evening meals, conversations and social events. Managing this expectation and living with the reality of it can be quite a chore; some parents report that it's like having a cross between a teenage daughter and a new puppy. In an ideal world she will embrace her new job, ask for guidance when required and perform her duties to your satisfaction. In the real world things can be rather different. The language barrier for some is a challenge and a source of entertainment; for others it may be the difference between instructions being understood or ignored. The best thing you can do in that situation is to explain instructions verbally and in writing, using simple vocabulary and grammar, and have a dictionary always close at hand. Ask her to repeat things back to you to make sure she has understood, and remember that the best way to teach someone practical skills, like operating kitchen appliances, is to show them, let them do it, then allow them to get on with it.

Having your new au pair babysit for the first time can be a leap of faith, but most families have an idea of their au pair's common sense and capability when they first leave her alone with the children. If you are unsure about when to take this step, arrange an evening when you are either in the house and out of sight or next door and within easy reach so that she can practise her babysitting skills but, if need be, call on you.

As well as learning English and helping you with the children and housework, your au pair won't have forgotten the small matter of weekly pay. Even though you may see her as an extra mouth to feed and a teenager who needs managing, you can't withhold pocket money as you might with your own children. If she has a bank account, you can arrange weekly payment by standing order. Although her salary will normally include two nights' babysitting a week, any extra should be paid at the usual hourly rate for your area.

Accommodating someone from outside the family in your home is always going to have its ups and downs, and au pairs need time to adjust to a new culture and language. One mother who employed a Swedish au pair had to give her some discreet advice on covering up a bit more, as she was from a family who, by all accounts, went around the house very scantily clad . . .

Another reports that her au pair only seemed to shower once a week: 'I did bite the bullet in the end and suggest it might be a good example to the kids to take a shower every day, but it was a difficult conversation!' Yet another had the opposite problem with an Italian girl who was a joy to have around in many ways but regularly used up all the hot water (and spent a lot of her time talking loudly on the phone). On the language side, a Bulgarian au pair was unused to the inversion of verb and subject in forming a question in English: 'Instead of "can you" or "will you" she would say "you can" or "you will". So you can imagine my husband didn't react too well when she tried to ask him if he would be back by seven that evening. "You will be back by seven," she commanded – sounding rather like me in fact . . .!'

Au pairs may reinforce national stereotypes, of course, and accordingly families may be prone to asking for particular nationalities or even religions when dealing with an agency. One agency is constantly deluged with requests for Scandinavians, while another has a regular demand for Catholics. The idea is that Catholic girls will be demure, hardworking and not have boyfriends to stay, but that's not always the case . . .

WHEN THINGS GO WRONG

When you have gone to all the trouble of welcoming and embracing your new au pair into the bosom of your family, when you have been at pains to speak in simple English and make her life comfortable in every possible way, problems in your relationship can leave you reeling. Why isn't she grateful? Why isn't it working? Where did you go wrong?

The most delightful-sounding girl can turn out to have a whole new side once she has her feet under your table. Helen has employed six au pairs in total, including short-term summer placements, with some disasters. Her German au pair, Eva, was efficient to the point of ruthlessness, told the children off constantly and usually in front of the parents, 'making me feel like a really hopeless mother apart from anything else', and her experience of a French nanny remains etched on her memory: 'She would insist on wearing this awful perfume, and not just a whiff of a spray but it seemed like gallons of the stuff.' Mary's Slovenian girl ate them out of house and home – 'a whole packet of ham in her sandwich, six sausages at one sitting . . .'

In some cases there is nothing you can do about a problem with an au pair. If the children take an inexplicable dislike to her, if she proves to be a completely incompetent cook, if she lacks initiative, there will be little you can do to remedy the situation. Claire's first au pair was unable to control her two boisterous boys, and Claire was rarely able to leave the kitchen at mealtimes for fear of a riot breaking out. But some parents find that time and attention, listening to the au pair's point of view, can go a long way to solving a problem.

Here are some top tips from parents who have had au pairs and learnt the hard way.

- Don't expect miracles; be grateful for an extra pair of hands.
- Give her the rules at the outset. It's hard to introduce new ones as you go along because she will take it as criticism of the way she has done something.
- Buy a basic, easy recipe book and, if necessary, do the

shopping yourself so there is no excuse for her not producing nice meals for the children.

- Make sure she understands the rules about use of phone and computer. Most au pairs have mobiles but many a family has seen bills go up astronomically with a homesick au pair in the house.
- If you prefer to eat separately as a couple, let her join you on, say, one night a week. Eating with the children is fine, but she needs to know she is accepted as one of the adults too.
- Make sure she knows whether and when it's okay to have guests and whether and when her family is welcome.
- Be direct about approaching problems. The language barrier can make any subtlety completely pointless.

Everyone knows a horror story about an au pair. I have heard of one mother finding a shrine to her husband in the au pair's wardrobe: hair from his brush, a used razor blade – yes, really! But it is always the horror stories that make the headlines, and for every disaster there are likely to be hundreds of happy and functioning relationships across the country. Susie, a divorced mother of two and full-time working solicitor, cannot praise her lovely French au pair highly enough: 'Where can I start? Words simply do not exist to describe what a complete godsend Sara has been. Just seeing her smiling face every morning over the breakfast table, the way she really brings her youth and enthusiasm into the children's lives, they way she thinks of what needs doing without being told, I'll miss her so much when she goes!'

Laura has had three Swedish au pairs in the last three years and is similarly full of praise: 'I know you shouldn't generalise but . . . their English is so good, they are so helpful, so active, energetic, sporty and sort of clean-living. A real breath of fresh air. My children have learnt some Swedish – although I can't see that being much use if all Swedes are so good at English.'

So, the message about au pairs is that you may be lucky, but do as much homework as you can in order to avoid finding something sinister in the cupboard . . . For first-time host families, using an agency to assist with the process is proven to increase the success rate. Ask the agency to explain how they recruit, match and support, and what they do if things go wrong; every agency should have terms for you to see prior to signing up.

Nicole Kofkin, managing director of Smart Au Pairs, comments on the au-pair experience: 'I'm Dutch, and I was lucky to learn four European languages at school. I enjoyed travelling and languages from a young age and had an exciting career in international travel marketing for more than 10 years. Hosting an au pair for my young children was a natural thing to do. Every au pair was very different, yet all were an amazing addition to our family for a year. I knew that running an au-pair agency would give me the opportunity to enthuse other families about "cultural childcare" and give au pairs the chance to "earn and learn". Now many families return to our agency year after year and au pairs return home and email me that they are helping to prepare the profile for a younger sister or for several friends to travel next year!

'I see so many applications from amazing young people wishing to broaden their horizons – from a 19-year-old black-belt karate pro from Germany, who had volunteered with deprived children to help them with confidence and discipline, to a Spanish nursery-school teacher who went to university evening classes to qualify as an English teacher and arrived in Britain armed with a notebook with everything from children's songs to Spanish cuisine. Needless to say, both made amazing au pairs.'

BABYSITTERS

'Babysitter' is another word that may be misused and misunderstood between cultures. Some people use the term 'babysitting' to cover any type of childcare, and indeed it does have a more general interpretation. For the purposes of this book, a babysitter is a responsible adult (usually over 16) who looks after children in the evenings when the parents are out. Most agencies will call any childcare after 7 p.m. babysitting, often because their babysitters have day jobs from which they need to return and recover before starting the next shift.

THE ALTERNATIVE TO A BABYSITTER – LEAVING YOUR CHILD ALONE . . .

How do you decide if you can safely leave a child alone? There is no legal provision on the age at which children may be left alone at home but there are many important things to consider before you decide to do so. These include:

- the age of the child
- the child's level of maturity and understanding
- the place where the child will be left
- how long the child will be alone, and how often
- whether or not there are any other children with the child

For example, most parents wouldn't think twice about leaving a 16-year-old alone for the evening, but wouldn't consider leaving them for a week.

AGE LIMIT AND QUALIFICATIONS

Babysitters do not need qualifications or a certificate to look after children and there is no legal minimum age, but the NSPCC recommends that the minimum age of a babysitter should be 16, which is also the age at which they become legally responsible.

CHOOSING A BABYSITTER – TOP TIPS FROM THE NSPCC

When deciding to use a babysitter remember to:

- choose someone aged over 16
- follow your instincts: if in doubt, don't use them (babysitter, not instincts!)
- ask for at least two references and contact the referees yourself
- speak to the babysitter's parents, if he/she lives at home with them
- listen to your child: talk to them about any babysitting issue they are unhappy about
- if your child is unhappy with a particular babysitter, find someone else

WHERE TO FIND A BABYSITTER

How you go about looking for a babysitter will depend on a number of factors, including the age(s) of your child(ren), any special needs, the hours you want covered, etc. Your neighbour's 16-year-old son may not be the right choice for a newborn baby but may be very popular with older children. If you are lucky enough to have a street full of competent teenagers looking for extra pocket money, and your requirements are standard and uncomplicated, you may need to look no further, but there are a number of other routes to try.

Agency Most nanny agencies operate a babysitting register; you pay an annual fee and they supply you with the contact details of a number of babysitters in your area who meet your requirements.

Babysitting circle These operate all over the UK, mostly in urban areas, and involve a system of babysitting by reciprocation. All members of the babysitting circle are allocated a certain number of tokens at the outset and use them to pay other members on an hourly basis. If cost is an issue this may be the perfect solution, but you will have to give up the odd precious Saturday night to sit alone in someone else's house. Also, your children may be in the hands of a mum or dad they have never met before. To find out more about babysitting circles in your area, contact your local branch of the National Childbirth Trust (NCT) who can usually put you in touch with a local co-ordinator.

Advertising In your local newsagent's window or library, and answering adverts you find there.

Websites Look at the usual childcare recruitment sites (see Resources, page 323) and consider placing your own advert for a regular sitter.

Recommendation Ask around for recommendations, but be aware that not everyone wants to share their babysitter with you if that means she will be less available for them!

Sarah and Giles found their fabulous babysitter through a card in the local paper shop. They are the natural parents of Jake and the adoptive parents of Michael, who suffers with ADHD.

> *It's been hard with Michael, and although his condition is controlled by medication, there aren't many people we can leave him with. We really need to spend time together as a couple to give ourselves the energy to be good parents (and I do like a night out!). We put a card up in the local newsagent's advertising for a babysitter and Clare rang us the next day. She was a special-needs teacher, a driver with her own car, and not much of a social life. Ideal! She was wonderful with both the boys and they soon really warmed to her. We have used her for years now – we have left them with her for the odd weekend and she comes and helps me in the holidays when she has time off.*

Fran economised by using her cleaner, which turned out to have other cost implications . . .

> *Marta was cheap and cheerful and did the ironing at the same time, so it seemed to make perfect sense for her to be our regular babysitter. Chloe (aged 10) used to groan when we announced Marta was babysitting but we ignored it, putting it down to her not wanting her parents to go out. But once when Chloe was at a sleepover party and Marta only*

had the younger two, she [Marta] was on the phone to us in tears because she couldn't get them to go to bed. We were amazed as this was the first time there had been a problem in five years. The next day Chloe came home and pointed out very matter-of-factly that she had always helped Marta get the other two to bed, because otherwise they would just run riot. I felt like the absolute worst mother in the world and have since registered with a local agency, which has supplied me with some much more professional alternatives to the lovely but useless Marta!

HOW TO GET THE MOST FROM YOUR BABYSITTER

Money Pay your babysitter the going rate. This may range from £5 to £10 per hour depending on where you live, the age and experience of the babysitter. Most babysitters charge a standard rate similar to, although usually slightly less than, the current standard hourly rate for a nanny. Make sure you are aware of the rate your babysitter is going to charge before you invite him or her to work for you. There may be room for negotiation, but generosity breeds generosity and if you think you have found a good one, you may have to pay top whack to secure their services. As a guideline, it is polite to offer a babysitter time-and-a-half after midnight, and to offer to pay the cost of a cab home if he or she doesn't drive.

Planning Babysitters like plenty of notice, and hate cancellations. It is polite to give as much notice as possible of any cancellation, and cancelling a weekend babysit with less than 24 hours' notice should warrant some compensation. Most agencies recommend a minimum payment for an evening, and request a late-cancellation fee for babysitters of around three hours' money. Frequent cancellation without compensation can lead to your babysitter becoming mysteriously busy just when you need him next time . . .

Refreshments and entertainment Babysitters don't generally expect to be served dinner, but if he is going to be there from 7 p.m. till 1 a.m., it is polite to offer him the wherewithal to make a sandwich. If you are aware that you aren't paying top rates but want to keep him happy, this may be one way in which you can do that. As a rule, though, you shouldn't have to provide more than tea- and coffee-making facilities and a tin of biscuits. He will expect to be able to use your TV, so show him how to do that, but you shouldn't have to give him access to the computer or the phone.

Safety issues Ideally, your babysitter should have done some kind of first-aid course, but since most parents aren't first-aid trained, we don't expect the 16-year-old next door to be. However, you do need to be reassured that your babysitter knows everything they need to know about safety in the home while you are out. Even if he has a set of emergency numbers to call, phones can be engaged and reception disrupted. It is vital that he has all the information he needs to deal with an emergency. Most such information will only have to be given once, but it's useful to have the list in case you use a different babysitter on a particular occasion.

Overleaf is a safety checklist to consult each time you use a new babysitter.

- Allow plenty of time before you leave to deliver all the safety information.
- Provide the babysitter with your mobile numbers, plus the mobile and landline numbers of any emergency contacts.
- Introduce him to the family pets.
- Show him the first-aid box and location of the fire extinguisher/torch/candles. Make sure the first-aid box is fully stocked and that he is aware of when and how to administer any medicine.
- Make sure he understands how to put the baby down to sleep, and all the safe-sleep guidelines.
- Make sure he understands how to deal with a baby who won't stop crying.
- If he is going to feed the children, make sure he is familiar with food-safety guidelines – how to feed a baby safely and how to deal with choking.
- Tell him about locking windows and doors, and any outside lights.
- He should check on the children regularly if they are asleep.
- Make sure he understands that he should not let anyone into the house unless he personally knows him or her *and* that you have given permission.
- Make sure he understands not to identify himself as a babysitter on the phone, but that he should say you (the parent) can't come to the phone and take a message.
- Advise him not to use the phone in case you are trying to call.
- Make sure he is aware he should never leave a child alone in the bath, not even for a second.

- In case of fire, make sure he knows all the ways out of the house and how he will get the children out.

Your sitter will need lots of general information from you before you leave. Allow enough time to go over the information, show them the house and answer any questions. Again, it is useful to have a checklist on a notice-board in the kitchen so that whoever happens to be babysitting has easy access to everything they need to know. The list should include:

- parents' names and mobile numbers
- full address of the house and landline number
- details of the location of the house (for example, which road it is off, if there are any landmarks nearby) in case he needs to give directions to emergency services
- name and phone number of GP
- emergency services number (999)
- name and phone number of neighbours and close relatives – include a few in case some contacts are not at home
- list any food and drug allergies
- any special medical information, such as asthma, etc.
- where you will be – name, address and phone number
- children's bedtimes and bedtime routine
- any other special instructions

The final thing to remember about babysitters is, don't close the door to new ones. The most regular and reliable sitters may have social engagements on the very day you most need them – students go off to university, people move away, or can even come down with flu the night before the office party you so want to go to. My children are now all of school age, and have a distinct preference for young, trendy babysitters and nannies over older, experienced (and stricter) alternatives. I tend to use local teenagers, who win them over and are actually much better at getting them into bed than Granny is. Keep an up-to-date list of sitters, with their mobile numbers on your phone. Most importantly, if you want to retain their loyalty, pay them well, give them lots of notice, don't cancel at the last minute and invest heavily in chocolate Hobnobs.

SUMMARY

Before taking on an au pair, have you considered that:

- she will not be as experienced or necessarily as capable as a nanny?
- her working hours are restricted?
- she should not look after babies?
- she is unlikely to stay for more than a year?
- you will have to treat her as a member of your family?
- that there will be language barrier and other cultural issues?

The success of the au-pair scheme in the UK is testament to its ongoing popularity with parents who appreciate the extra pair of hands and built-in babysitter at such a low cost. As with any form of home-based childcare, especially live-in, there will be a relationship to maintain and nurture, but most employers of au pairs find that the investment is well worth the trouble.

CHAPTER 7

Childminders

Registered childminders are self-employed professional day-carers who work in their own homes to provide care and education for other people's children in a family setting. Unlike nannies and au pairs, they must be registered under the 1989 Children Act by Ofsted in England, or by the Care and Social Services Inspectorate Wales (CSSIW).

With the inception of the National Childminding Association (NCMA) and the hard work of local authorities, there has been a decline in casual use of unregistered carers in their own homes, and now it is illegal for a childminder to work without having applied for registration; if she does so, she may be prosecuted. (Parents who use unregistered childminders are not liable to be prosecuted.) Local authorities across the country work closely with childminders to provide varying degrees of practical support (from training courses and drop-in centres to loan of high-chairs and travel cots) and encourage all childminders to become members of the NCMA and reap the benefits of that membership.

Childminders are still the most popular form of childcare in Britain. There are more than 100,000 registered childminders in England and Wales, caring for up to 500,000 children at any one time.

A childminder may be the right option for you if:

- you want your child to be cared for in a home environment
- you want your child to be cared for by one person only
- you have children of different ages whom you wish to be cared for together in one place
- you want your child to socialise with others
- you are relaxed about being unable to choose the other children in the setting
- you need flexible care or work irregular hours
- you work from home and need childcare to be based away from home
- you have checked availability locally and there are vacancies
- cost is an issue for you

MYTHS AND REALITY

One of the most common misconceptions about childminders is that they are a cheap childcare option for the working classes and manual labourers. An image comes to mind of a large no-nonsense 50-something woman, fag in hand, curlers in hair, living in a cramped house escorting throngs of children in and out of the front door. The reality of childminders today is very different. Aside from anything else, they have to compete in the childcare market; and most children in the care of childminders live a much more healthy and outdoor lifestyle than they did in the past. Childminders must be registered, which means showing a certain commitment to a childcare career, most are mothers and many have additional childcare qualifications.

Anne is a childminder working in north Surrey. She has a three-year-old son and looks after three other children during the day.

> *I feel so lucky to be doing a paid job that actually includes my own little boy. I love being a mum at home but needed to work, and this makes perfect sense. We have so much baby-and-toddler equipment in the house, and the house is so child-safe anyway, that going through the motions of registration wasn't much of an effort. I love bringing the efficiency and creativity of my working persona into this very personal environment. It's like running your own mini child-care business, and I have so few clients that I can get them all involved in making decisions about our activities and outings. I realise that all these children could be going to the local nursery, but that the parents have chosen to use me instead. That gives me a sense of pride and responsibility, and I can't allow myself to ignore the trust and confidence they have in me.*

DUTIES

There are some things you can assume will fall within a childminder's remit, and some that you may have to negotiate. The way a childminder does things is likely to be well-ingrained, and the children already in that setting will be used to the routine, so you will have trouble making any significant changes. However, there is always some scope to cater for children's individual needs, so it's probably worth making a request if your requirements don't appear to be covered . . .

A childminder will:

- have sole charge of children in her own home
- provide nutritious meals, snacks and drinks throughout the day as appropriate
- provide age-appropriate activities and entertainment for the children in her care following the Early Years Foundation Stage Framework
- organise suitable activities to promote the development of children in her care

A childminder may:

- do school runs and offer before- and/or after-school care
- provide holiday-only care for additional children
- provide more flexible hours for childcare than a nursery
- allow overnight stays (more commonly in rural areas)

PLAYDATES

One of the disadvantages of using a childminder rather than a nanny is the difficulty of arranging playdates – when your child has another child over to play or vice versa. A childminder is already limited to a strict quota of children and may not be able to accommodate your child's friends for tea after school. Equally, she may not be able to fit journeys to other children's houses into her day. If your child has particular playdate favourites, or if you feel that he would benefit from having playdates with chosen friends, make sure you raise this with the childminder at the outset.

QUALIFICATIONS AND REGISTRATION

A childminder must be registered with Ofsted, which inspects her home regularly and carries out regular CRB checks on her and anyone else in the house over 16. After registration, a childminder is checked every one to three years to ensure she is continuing to provide a safe and suitable service.

All childminders in England and Wales (although not yet in Scotland and Northern Ireland) are required to complete a basic training course with their local authority, including first aid. Some also have other childcare qualifications (for example, an NVQ in Early Years Care and Education).

TYPICAL COSTS

You'll need to agree a contract with your childminder to cover hours, holidays, overtime and so on. As they are self-employed, childminders have the right to stipulate their fees. Fees vary from area to area but expect to pay anything from £3–7 an hour per child, depending on where you are in the UK. You will still pay if your child is sick or on holiday because your childminder will be keeping the place open, but you will not usually pay if your childminder is on holiday. In any case, make sure that holiday arrangements are set out clearly in the contract.

HOURS

Childminders normally work a 10–11-hour day but this will vary from individual to individual. Some childminders provide after-school care only, or after-school, plus morning drop-off.

AGES COVERED

A childminder may look after children of any age from babies to teenagers, but registration regulations only apply to care provided for children under eight.

Government regulations stipulate that a childminder is allowed to look after six children under the age of eight (under twelve in Scotland and Northern Ireland). Of those six, no more than three should be under five; of those three, no more than one should be under a year (exceptions are made for siblings).

Any care for children over the age of eight should not be allowed to adversely affect the care provided for children under eight.

PROS

- Childminders are registered and inspected regularly, and may have childcare qualifications.
- They are likely to be experienced childcarers and often have children of their own.
- They will probably live locally and know the area very well.
- They may offer flexible hours.
- They may be prepared to drop off or collect from nursery or school.
- Your child will have other children to play with.
- They will be cared for in a small group.
- They will be in a home environment and will be involved in normal family activities.
- They will probably have continuity of care, especially if the childminder is prepared to do after-school hours, and will be looked after for several years by the same person (unlike in a nursery).
- The childminder can sometimes offer flexibility in a routine, unlike a nursery which is more geared to a strict timetable.
- They may be able to adapt activities to children with special needs.
- Childminders may become life-long friends.
- A childminder is less expensive than other childcare options.

CONS

- The childminder may want to organise her daily routine to suit her lifestyle rather than yours.
- It is more difficult to arrange playdates with her than it would be with a nanny.
- She is likely to be dealing with a range of ages – you must decide if this is suitable for your child.
- She may not be as flexible about hours as a nanny.
- Your child may take some time to settle into what is effectively a new 'home'.
- The childminder may not be prepared to drop off or collect from nursery or school.
- They probably won't be able to look after your child if he is ill.
- You may prefer to have your child(ren) looked after on their own.
- The childminder has her own chores to do so your child will get less one-to-one undivided attention than he would with a nanny.

TYPICAL DAY

As with a nanny, a childminder's typical day will vary enormously depending on where she works, how many children she looks after and their ages. A childminder with lots of school and nursery runs will be more limited in her flexibility than one who cares for mainly babies and toddlers. Some childminders work with others, sometimes in mother-and-daughter set-ups, which can facilitate school runs: babies don't have to be woken from naps to be bundled into prams, and preschoolers can benefit more from the home-based childcare setting without having to adapt to the older children's day.

All childminders should have a daily or weekly planner available for you to see what they get up to and how they are implementing the Early Years Foundation Stage Framework or, in plain English, how they are educating your child in accordance with government standards.

Typically, a childminder will give children breakfast when they arrive, then involve them in various activities during the morning where they learn from each other, by a method known as 'scaffolding'. The older children help the younger ones with scissors and Sellotape in art activities, and in a cooking activity the different jobs will be shared among the children as appropriate to their age. Children will learn as they go along at different levels, whether it's seeing solid chocolate melting and becoming solid again, or tying shoelaces.

Carol, a London childminder, likes to make learning fun, using themes that the children bring up themselves: 'Last week one of the children had been to the dentist, so we talked about teeth, looked at each other's teeth, discussed how to look after them and built a mini-project out of it.'

Most childminders will provide a cooked lunch, which the children may help with, followed by naps for the younger children while the older ones engage in quiet activities, such as drawing, puzzles or Play-Doh.

Spending time with children of other ages can develop sensitivity and thoughtfulness in children, and childminders often report that this setting is much more conducive to good sharing skills than others.

HOW TO FIND A REGISTERED CHILDMINDER

The best place to start is by asking people you know. Tell colleagues, friends and family that you are looking for a childminder. They may be able to recommend someone. But at the end of the day it's your decision, and what's right for your neighbour may not be right for you. Remember to start early: some parents are lucky enough to find their ideal childminder almost straight away while others take several months, and the best childminders usually have waiting lists. Contact your local Family Information Service (see Resources, pages 320–22) and ask for a list of registered childminders with vacancies in your area.

Before you visit a childminder, make a list of what you're looking for in a registered childminder. Think about things like:

- working hours
- fees
- discipline policies
- activities
- school and nursery runs
- food
- transport arrangements

Draw up a list of questions to ask them (see page 193).

Call some childminders and make appointments to visit them. You may want to make a short visit while they are childminding to watch them at work, and a longer visit one evening or weekend when they will probably have more time to discuss things.

MEETING YOUR CHILDMINDER

When you meet your childminder, there are certain checks you should make as a matter of course. Don't be embarrassed about asking what may seem intrusive questions or even nosiness. They will be used to it and you will probably go up in their estimation if you are keen to check that everything is in order. Make sure you shop around: don't plump for the first one you meet because she talks about being very booked up. Alice did exactly that:

> *The very first childminder I went to see told me she had one space left for September and several other parents coming to see her in the next few days. I felt under real pressure to accept the place, and did so, paying a deposit on the spot. Because I was new to it all I didn't know any better. The next woman I went to visit was so impressive that I realised I'd made a real mistake with the first. I ended up paying a second deposit but at least I know I've got the right person, and nothing is more important than that.*

Ideally you should not take your child along to your first meeting with the childminder – as with a nanny, it's much easier to gauge whether she's the right person if you aren't distracted by the antics of your own offspring. If you decide she's worth a second visit, take your child along and see how well the childminder deals with him. She should show plenty of interest in him and ask a lot of questions about him; his personality, likes and dislikes and current routine, as well as any past childcare experiences.

When interviewing a childminder, as with a nanny, pay attention not just to what she says in response to your questions but to how she answers them. If she is dismissive or flippant about an area of childcare that you feel strongly about, take this as a sign of her attitude to it. It's not enough that she has a cupboard bursting with toys; you want to know that she will get them out and play with them with your children. Similarly, try to assess the environment she works in: imagine your child spending his days there. An immaculate house may be a sign that messy play isn't at the top of her list of activities. As well as formal documents relating to Ofsted inspections and qualifications, most childminders will show you a portfolio of photos of them with their charges, letters of thanks from children and parents, and artwork and projects they have worked on with children, all of which helps to bring the setting to life.

Here are some essential points for the first visit.

- Ask to see her most recent registration certificate.
- Ask whether all rooms and the garden are insured or your child will be excluded from those areas.
- Check that the house seems spacious, clean and tidy (but not too tidy – you will want to see plenty of evidence of children around!).
- Look at the sleeping arrangements for daytime naps.
- Look at arrangements for nappy changing.
- Note whether or not the TV is on.
- Ask for the phone numbers of other parents you can speak to.
- Take note of what your gut is telling you.

QUESTIONS TO ASK YOUR CHILDMINDER

You will have a good instinct about what to ask a childminder, as you would with any childcare provider, but a list can make it less stressful and prove useful if you dry up in the heat of the moment. There's nothing worse than coming away from an interview remembering all the things you should have asked. So, here is your basic list of questions. You may not want to ask them all (it may take far too long) but they cover more or less everything you will need to know.

- What qualifications does she have, if any?
- How long has she been a childminder? Has she worked in any other childcare settings?
- What does she like about the job, and how long does she intend to stay in it?
- What ages are the children she currently looks after?
- Does she look after any children of her own? Can you meet them?
- What are the ages of the children she has looked after in the past? Ask about particular experience with children of your child's age.
- Who, if anyone, works with her? Find out about their qualifications and experience.
- If she has assistants, what is staff turnover like? How many staff have left in the last year?
- When was the most recent Ofsted inspection? What rating did the setting receive (outstanding, good, satisfactory or inadequate)?
- Has she joined any childminder networks or quality-assurance schemes?

- Does she charge for sick days?
- What is the daily routine, roughly?
- How does she fit in her own chores and shopping?
- What are her views on TV and other 'downtime'?
- What are her views on discipline and rewards?
- What kind of meals does she cook?
- Does she keep a diary or file about children's progress?
- Does she do day trips? If so, to what sort of places?
- Does she take children to playgroups and activities outside the home?
- Does she drive with the children she cares for and can she show you her car and car seats/booster seats?
- Does she do 'trial days' for new families?
- What is her settling-in policy?
- Which other adults, if any, come and go to and from the premises during the day?
- When and how would she expect to be paid?
- What happens about holiday?
- What is her accident/emergency policy?
- Can you pop in during the day to see your children?
- Is there any flexibility on school pick-up times – for instance, if your child attends an after-school club?

SPECIAL NEEDS

As well as all the usual considerations you will take into account when choosing a childminder, you may also need to think about questions like:

- Does the childminder have experience in looking after a child with a similar disability, and if not, would she be happy for you to show her what's needed?
- How much specialist care does your child need and is appropriate training available locally?
- Does your child have therapy or appointments they need to go to in the time they will be cared for and, if so, can your childminder take him to these appointments?
- Does the childminder need specialist training or equipment? Often childminders have to have had specific training to give medication. As a parent, you'll be shown how to give medication to your child by your doctor, nurse or health visitor. You can ask the same person to give this training to your child's new childminder.

See also Resources, pages 328–30.

WILL YOUR CHILD FIT IN?

As well as finding out if the childminder is right for you and your child, it's important to make sure your child is a good fit with the childminder. Find out what kind of behaviour she finds unacceptable, or difficult to deal with. How far, if at all, does your child fit into that category? Find out how she deals with any relevant type of behaviour. You don't want to discover that she hates shouting when you have a child who shouts all the time (I have one of those!).

REFERENCES

Word-of-mouth recommendation from other parents is a good guide to quality. Asking the childminder to give you the names of two parents to phone for a confidential chat will give you some extra reassurance.

CONTRACTS WITH CHILDMINDERS

When you have found the right childminder, take the time to complete a childminding contract together. This should cover hours, fees, food, transport, holiday and sickness arrangements, and anything else that's important to you. NCMA publishes contracts especially designed for parents and childminders to use and has the following advice for parents:

> *A written contract sets out clearly what is expected from the childminder, and what is expected from the parents, which can avoid disagreements later on. The contract also fulfils another very important function. No matter how little or well you know each other, it is important to begin your childminding relationship in a professional way. Even if you feel a bit uncomfortable talking about money and your personal childcare preferences, it is important that you do so. Taking an hour to fill in a childminding contract gives you a formal framework so that you are free to talk about these issues in a friendly but professional manner.*

As well as your contract, you will need to sign permission forms in certain circumstances, just as you will for school trips later, giving the childminder the authority to do certain things with your child, including routine outings, taking him or her in a car or on other transport, applying sun cream, administering medication, etc. Your childminder should be able to download standard permission forms from the NCMA website for these occasions.

REVIEWING YOUR CONTRACT

As the children grow older and circumstances change, it will be important to review the contract. NCMA recommends that you do so every six to twelve months. This means you also get a chance to talk about the children's progress and how things are going. Sometimes interesting issues can arise at these sessions. Kate says:

> *I had been using my childminder for about six months, dropping my two little boys off there at 7.45 a.m. and collecting them at 6 p.m. They were very happy to go there every day, but I did wonder why they seemed to be so desperate to eat before we left the house. I used to say they had to wait and eat breakfast at the childminder's house. They were only two and three at the time so they couldn't say much back to me. How awful did I feel when I found out at our annual review meeting that the childminder had always presumed the boys had breakfast at home! I was mortified, embarrassed, couldn't believe that we had gone on so long without knowing they were missing a meal every day. My advice is, don't make any assumptions about what's included in the contract.*

SETTLING IN

Settling a child with a childminder can be harder than it is with a new nanny because the setting is an unfamiliar house. Children need to get to know a childminder and other children in her care gradually. You may want to accompany your child on a first visit, then make another short visit, popping out for a few minutes, leaving your child with the childminder. This should help him to settle in more easily when he starts going to the childminder regularly. When you hand your child over in the mornings, the best tactic is to do so decisively and leave promptly. It's not unusual for a child to be very clingy on the doorstep and to cry at first when he is left but this should change with time.

KEEPING A GOOD RELATIONSHIP WITH YOUR CHILDMINDER

You can maintain a good working relationship with your childminder by communicating regularly about your child's development, discussing any problems as soon as they arise, bringing and collecting your child on time, paying fees on time and letting the childminder know that their work is valued. Vicky says:

I have had the same childminder for my two children for the last six years, since the youngest was six months old. Jean is like part of our family, like an extra granny almost. It hasn't all been amazing and perfect – we have had our little misunderstandings and have had to learn about each other and make the odd compromise, as you have to in any relationship, but I have really noticed that investing in the relationship has paid off, and the continuity of care has been brilliant for our girls. It's like a second home for them. Jean has her own grown-up children and has that great combination of experience and common sense from being a mother and a granny herself, and that playfulness you want in someone looking after your children. She was brilliant with them as babies, and is just as good now they're at school, helping them become more independent and responsible. I think having to look after children of different ages simultaneously means she's always in tune with their different needs and stages of development. I would recommend childminders to anyone.

WHAT TO DO IF THERE'S A PROBLEM

The NCMA guidelines give you a clear idea of the type and level of service you should expect from a childminder. If you have any concerns about the level of care, you should raise them with the childminder in the first instance. Many issues can be resolved at an early stage and may have resulted from a misunderstanding. If you have already approached your childminder, and still don't feel they are providing an adequate level of care, you can contact the Ofsted complaints line. If a child's safety is at risk, or there is any concern about a child-protection issue, you should remove your child immediately and contact the Child Protection Team at your local Social Services.

The NCMA has the following advice for avoiding disputes.

- Agree a signed contract at the start of your arrangement to make sure both you and the childminder are clear about what is expected.
- Take time to discuss issues – for example, what happens if the childminder, child or parent is ill, or what will happen if the parent is late picking up the child, at the start of the relationship rather than when it actually happens. Keep talking. Raising concerns as they arise can prevent problems building up.
- Share information. Keeping one another up to date with what's happening in the child's life can be important in helping them to feel settled and the childminder to offer the best care. Many childminders and parents use a daily journal to share information – you may let the childminder know that your child had a restless night so may be tired today, while the childminder may let you know that your child managed to tie his shoelaces . . .

SUMMARY

Before engaging a childminder, have you considered:

- why you prefer this option over other types of childcare?
- your views on childcare outside the home?
- the social implications (other children cared for, limits on playdates)?
- the reputation, references and Ofsted reports relevant to the setting?

All the people I spoke to when I was researching this book had nothing but good things to say about childminders. Apart from the misunderstanding about breakfast, and a badly drafted contract that was unclear on the issue of holiday pay, the overall feedback was very positive. In particular, parents praised childminders' flexibility, versatility, warmth, value for money and general reliability. Childminders, it seems, rarely take days off sick, and often belong to a strong local network, which gives them practical and moral support. They also seem to be a happy bunch, describing themselves as happy, or very happy, doing the work they do. No wonder, then, that this is the nation's most popular childcare option.

CHAPTER 8

Day Nurseries, Workplace Childcare and Children's Centres

DAY NURSERIES

A day nursery is a daycare setting open all year round which must be registered with Ofsted, or the equivalent government regulatory body, and is inspected every year. There are more than 15,000 day nurseries in the UK where more than 675,000 children are cared for.

Day nurseries vary in size. Children are usually grouped together according to age and will follow a government-approved early-years curriculum. Most will care for children between the ages of three months and five years, although a few will take children up to eight and beyond, using a school drop-off system, after-school and holiday clubs. Some will take babies from as young as six weeks. All have a designated special educational needs co-ordinator (SENCo) to manage provision for children with special needs.

A day nursery may be the right choice for your child if:

- you want somewhere open year round
- your working hours fit with the opening times
- you are happy with childcare outside the home
- you feel more comfortable about there being lots of qualified staff around
- you want your child to socialise

MYTHS AND REALITY

Nurseries have come a long way, even in the last 10 years, and the vision of cluttered, overcrowded rooms in badly converted town-houses is becoming a thing of the past. Another image, of over-sterile, clinical institutions completely lacking in warmth and atmosphere, is rarely to be found. The 'hot cotting' approach to putting babies to sleep is no longer the norm, with more and more nurseries allocating specific sleeping provision for specific children rather than getting one up as the next goes down for a nap. Today's nurseries are more likely to be purpose-built, carefully designed buildings with plenty of outdoor space and all mod cons. It's a competitive market and any nursery that doesn't pass muster with parents will soon find that reflected in its profit figures. I have seen nurseries designed by *feng-shui* consultants, with murals commissioned from local artists, toddler toothbrushes lined up by the washbasins for post-prandial teeth-cleaning, and even a sound-proofed room for orchestra practice (orchestra meaning percussion group, I think!). In another departure from the norm, some nurseries also offer a babysitting service, with nursery staff taking your children home and putting them to bed if you will be back late.

Nurseries have to be good to attract the best staff. Qualified childcarers will always go where they feel that pay and conditions match what they deserve, and nurseries are keeping up with that demand. Naturally this is reflected in the price you pay, and it would seem, from an overview of what is available nationwide, that you really do get what you pay for. But are parents prepared to foot the bill for what they might consider luxuries? Jane MacIntyre was forced to close down her nursery business in Glasgow because it seemed that her customers didn't want that level of service from a nursery. She had better luck elsewhere: 'I knew that with my own children I would want a level of care and attention that would merit the extra cost, and I was already squeezing my profit margin as tight as I could, but it just seems that in some areas there is a certain price you can't go above. When we opened in a more upmarket area two years later, there was a waiting list within months!'

It remains a problem for many nurseries that there is a high turnover of staff and absenteeism, leading to a certain lack of continuity for children. The high turnover can be partly attributed to nurseries being squeezed on salaries by what parents will pay, and the corresponding – tempting – increase in nanny salaries, which causes many nursery nurses to defect to private homes, Absenteeism is a common problem in nurseries, as illnesses are passed around like wildfire, and staff are often in close proximity to infection. Another inevitable consequence of caring for several babies in one place is, in the words of one nursery nurse, 'When one starts crying, all the others start, the sleeping ones wake up, and it can take a long time to get quiet again!'

The important thing is to be as fully informed as possible before discounting the nursery option. One mother told me, 'I was absolutely against the idea of nurseries to start with – for some reason they made me think of orphanages. I imagined them run by bored teenagers and populated by screaming babies, institutional food and no individual attention. I was absolutely amazed at what I found when I went to have a look at them. I saw lovely committed staff who really took an interest in the children, happy babies, lots of things going on and such a lovely atmosphere. I almost wanted to work there (just for a split second!).'

Nurseries have been the focus of a major childcare revolution and have a tremendous amount to offer the modern family. Carers spend a lot of time compiling reports, doing observations and assembling and displaying the children's creations, their first pictures and written work. Timetables include music, singing, messy and outdoor play, as well as reading, writing and computer work as the children get older. Variety and opportunity are everything. Seeing really is believing.

QUALIFICATIONS AND STAFFING IN NURSERIES

Nurseries are required to meet minimum staffing levels. Regular volunteers can be included in these staff ratios, but students on short-term placements cannot. These staffing levels must be maintained during outings, and in some circumstances it may be necessary for the nursery to have more staff available. There must be suitable arrangements in place to maintain staff–child ratios during staff holidays, sickness, emergencies, etc. At least half of the staff must hold relevant childcare qualifications, such as NVQ Childcare Level 2 or equivalent, and one member of staff should have a first-aid certificate. All supervisors are required to have an NVQ Childcare Level 3 or equivalent.

PROS

- A day nursery will be registered and inspected regularly.
- It is set up for the safety, care and education of young children.
- It will probably fit in well with your work or study hours.
- It will usually be open all year (although some close for short periods).
- Your child will be cared for by experienced carers.
- Your child will have an appropriate and structured learning programme.
- Your child will be among children of her own age.
- There is no wear and tear on your home as care takes place outside the home.

CONS

- Your child may be cared for by several carers, although most nurseries operate a 'key worker' system, whereby each child is assigned to a particular member of staff.
- Your child won't be in her own home.
- The hours may not be as flexible as you need, for instance if you do night shifts.

- The fees may be high, although support to pay them may be available through tax credits, depending on your income – and there is statutory provision for free nursery places for all three- and four-year-olds (see website for up-to-date information on this).
- Waiting lists can be long, especially for popular nurseries.
- You and your child may have to travel some distance.
- The staff won't be able to care for your child if she's ill.

TYPICAL DAY

What goes on in a nursery on a day-to-day basis will vary enormously, depending on the room (baby or toddler), the location of the nursery and its facilities (does it have a big garden or outdoor space, or is it near a park?) and the way in which the setting delivers the provision within the Early Years Foundation Stage Framework. Most nurseries will have a planner or wall chart available to parents so they can see what activities have been organised. Your child is likely to come home with mountains of artwork over the space of a year, some of it surprisingly adventurous. I remember being particularly impressed when my three-year-old brought home a beautiful collage made of pasta twists sprayed gold, and another occasion when my little boy, aged only one, did a painting of hand- and footprints – without a single speck of paint on his skin or clothes. One expects hygiene to be rigorous at a nursery, but I believe so should the adventurousness of activities – I always relished the idea that my children were engaging in the sort of seriously messy play at nursery that I just didn't have the appetite for in my immaculate kitchen.

TYPICAL COSTS

The typical cost of a full-time nursery place for a child under two is £167 a week in England; that's more than £8,600 a year (according to figures published in 2009). In some parts of the country, particularly London and the south east, the cost of a nursery place is much higher – from £226 up to £500 a week in some central London nurseries, or around £25,000 a year. The typical cost for a full-time nursery place for a child under two in Scotland is £158 and in Wales £146.

FINDING A DAY NURSERY

The first thing to do when looking at nurseries is to make sure you have all the options in front of you. This may require a fair bit of research, but the following will be your first ports of call (see Resources, pages 325–6, for contact details and useful websites):

- Childcare Link: the government website where you can search for all registered childcare including nurseries and childminders
- Family Information Service: run by your local council, offering information on all forms of childcare
- local telephone directory or yell.com: listings of local day nurseries
- your health visitor, doctor or the nurse at your surgery
- your employer: is there a workplace nursery?
- other parents

Bear in mind that good nurseries are booked up a very long time in advance, so to get what you want you will need to start early, in some cases as soon as you are pregnant. The one everyone's raving about may be fully subscribed and you may have to compromise on your choice, but consider keeping a place on the waiting list while you use another nursery, or hire a nanny on a temporary basis until the right vacancy comes up.

VISITING A NURSERY

Visiting local day nurseries can be time-consuming, and logistically difficult if you are bringing your baby and toddler with you. But it's worth doing a thorough investigation of what's on offer to be sure you make the right decision. You shouldn't expect to have to settle for anything less than complete peace of mind when it comes to leaving your child in daycare.

You will learn a lot from observing the nursery in action, but try to make sure you are shown round by someone who is able to answer some essential questions that will help you with your decision. Being shown round by the nursery owner is all very well but it can be much more enlightening if your guide is directly involved in managing or delivering the programme. Some of the questions listed opposite may sound intrusive – but you need to know the answers: your child's welfare depends on them.

An excellent nursery will be completely happy to show you around unannounced. If you visit without an appointment, you will know that you are seeing the nursery as it really is. If you sense any unwillingness to show you around unannounced, try another nursery.

QUESTIONS TO ASK/CONSIDER ON A VISIT TO A NURSERY

The staff

1. How many staff are qualified? In the best settings, all staff will have a recognised childcare qualification. A nursery with a high proportion of unqualified staff will probably not be putting child development first.
2. Exactly what qualifications do the staff have? How many have NVQ Level 3? Is a qualified teacher or early-years professional in charge of the educational provision (many of the best settings will offer this)?
3. What is staff turnover like? How many staff have left in the last year?
4. Do all staff get regular time away from the children for curriculum planning, discussing children's welfare, management supervision, etc? If so, how much? Are ratios maintained while this is happening?
5. Will your child have a key carer? How many children will that carer look after? What happens when they're off sick or on holiday?
6. Has every staff member's CRB check been completed? Can they prove this?
7. Do parents and staff work in partnership, recording your child's activities and achievements?

Seals of approval

1. When was the latest health and safety inspection? What rating did the nursery receive?
2. If the nursery is rated 'good' in its Ofsted report, note the recommendations for improvement in the report and be ready to ask the nursery whether these have been acted upon.

3. When was the last Ofsted inspection done? If not in the last 12 months, you will need to be reassured by the nursery that standards have not dropped since then.
4. Does the nursery belong to a professional organisation, such as the National Day Nurseries Association (NDNA), which will keep them informed of current issues?
5. Has the nursery gained any kite-marks of excellence, especially those endorsed by the government or Investors in Children, such as the NDNA's Quality Counts, Investors in People or Investors in Children?

Hygiene, happiness and safety

1. Is there a safe and clean outside play area?
2. Is the interior bright, warm, clean, well decorated and welcoming?
3. Is the equipment of good quality, clean, safe and appropriate?
4. What sort of meals are provided and at what time? Is the food fresh? Can they accommodate special diets? Are the menus changed regularly?
5. Do the children in the nursery look happy and occupied? Are they using a variety of equipment and are staff involved with their play?
6. Are the staff happy, relaxed, well presented, calm and confident?

Cost

What will the cost be and what does it include? For example, nappies, meals, French lessons, holiday charges, etc.

Policies and routines

1. Discuss activities such as potty training, emergency procedures and other nursery policies.
2. What are their policies on discipline and how do they manage children's behaviour?
3. Do they provide meals, snacks, nappies, etc., or will you need to provide them?
4. Where can the child sleep or rest?
5. How will they contact you in an emergency?
6. What clothes is your child expected to wear? Are there any extra items you need to supply, such as PE or swimming kit or art overalls?
7. What are the playtime and lunchtime arrangements? Is there some structure and will the children be supervised?
8. What are the toilet arrangements? And where are they located?
9. What skills does the nursery expect your child to have (for example, dressing and undressing, doing up own shoes)?

Your impressions

Did you enjoy your visit? Was it friendly, relaxed and informative? Did your child enjoy it?

SUMMARY OF WHAT YOU WILL FIND IN A GREAT NURSERY

- Trained and experienced staff, ready to learn and respond to your child's individual needs.
- Busy, but relaxed children, who seem happy and purposeful.

- Safe and clean premises, welcoming and friendly with outside play space.
- Cultural sensitivity and responsiveness to children's home life.
- A staff team and group of children who reflect local ethnic and cultural groups.
- Fun activities planned each day: childminders, nurseries and out-of-school clubs all need to plan their days with children's interests in mind.
- Exercise and quiet times to relax.
- A big welcome for you and your child.
- A good or outstanding Ofsted report.

If you are not happy with any aspect of the nursery, look elsewhere.

Jocelyn Ashton set up Building Blocks nursery in 2000, and her ethos is based on what she felt she wanted for her children at the time: 'You want your children to have an even better experience in their childcare setting than they would at home with you,' she says. 'Only then will you be able to go to work with complete peace of mind.' At Building Blocks, which boasts exceptional standards, exceptional staff retention (and exceptionally long waiting lists to match), she says she aims to achieve nothing less than excellence in childcare and education. Parents of children at Building Blocks know they are lucky to be there. Their children have the opportunity to do yoga, tumble gym, French, Spanish, dancing, drama and swimming, and that's just the beginning. Organic food, fun outings and webcams, which allow you to watch your child at play while you sit in your office, complete the picture of a daycare setting that delivers more than you could possibly expect.

OFSTED REGISTRATION AND INSPECTION

Always ensure that the nursery you choose is registered with Ofsted. The registration certificate should be displayed with a current certificate of insurance.

Ofsted reports are the official stamp of approval of any (registered) childcare setting. Inevitably, there is a certain amount of inconsistency across the board with inspections – one inspector may find fault with something to which another has no objection, but ideally you should only use childcare that Ofsted rates as 'outstanding' or 'good'. 'Satisfactory' may indicate serious concerns about some aspects of the childcare – and no parent needs to take that risk. If the nursery is rated 'good', you can investigate further by downloading the full report from the Ofsted website: www.ofsted.gov.uk. If the nursery is rated 'outstanding', this is a good indication that your child will receive very high-quality care and education at the nursery in question.

FINALLY . . . TAKE UP REFERENCES

I recommend that parents take up at least two references for any childcare provider and that includes nurseries. Childcare providers should be happy to give you the names and phone numbers of other parents to speak to about the service they provide.

CHILDREN'S VIEWS

What will your child enjoy? Children said that these things were most important when Daycare Trust visited nurseries and asked them for their views.

- Friends: check that a stable group of children attends so your children can have fun with friends.
- Food: check that mealtimes are relaxed and fun and ask if children can help themselves to drinks and snacks.
- Fun outside: check the outside area is well planned, spacious and safe – children love playing outdoors.
- Finding out: make sure there is plenty of opportunity for children to learn new things with varied, carefully planned activities.

The NDNA is a charity that aims to enhance the development and education of children in their early years through the provision of support services to members. All day nurseries that belong to the NDNA agree to its mission statement.

> *NDNA aims to enhance the development and education of children in their early years, through the provision of support services to members. It seeks to develop, encourage and maintain high standards in education and care for the benefit of the children, their families and their local communities.*

Many NDNA member nurseries have achieved the NDNA's Quality Counts accreditation or are working towards it. This comprehensive quality-assurance programme provides a kite-mark to inform parental choice of childcare and give reassurance and confidence about the quality of the setting.

PREPARING YOUR CHILD FOR NURSERY

As with any new childcare arrangement, you should allow some time for your child to settle in. At a childcare setting outside the home, this may mean staying with your child on his first visit, then leaving him for short periods on his own, building up to a full day.

Before his first day, you may want to check the following with the nursery or school:

- What is the 'official' settling-in procedure?
- Do they require your child to be toilet trained (depending on age)?
- Are there any routines you can practise in advance?

The first day at nursery is one of your child's biggest milestones. How he reacts will depend on his age and his life up to this point. If he's been at home all the time and he's over a year old, he may feel it's a huge change and it may take him a while to adjust, but if he's a baby and/or has already been in a form of childcare outside the home, he'll be prepared to some extent. However resilient he is, there are always practical things you can do at home to get your child ready for the big event.

- Talk together about going to nursery and listen to any worries he may have.
- Include him in shopping trips to buy any equipment he needs.

- Be upbeat and positive: don't pass any of your worries to your child.
- Explain the thrill of making new friends.
- Walk past the nursery when the children are playing happily outside.
- Explain what will happen during the day.
- Read books together about children starting nursery.
- Point out any friends or cousins who've recently started nursery and talk about the fun they're having.
- Talk about your child's interests and the things he'll enjoy there. For example: 'There'll be lots of sand to play with – you'll love that' or 'There'll be storytime.'
- Talk about the enjoyable activities he'll be doing that build on things he already does at home – painting, drawing, cutting and pasting, and listening to stories, for example.

SETTLING IN

Here are some of the practical ways in which you can help your child settle in to a new nursery as painlessly as possible.

- Point out the structure and routines in a day at home: 'Now it's our lunchtime and at nursery you'd be eating your lunch now.'
- Practise doing up buttons and fastening his shoes, but don't worry or pressure him if this proves too difficult. Nursery staff are used to helping children in the early days.
- Practise social skills, such as taking turns, following directions and making choices. Visit friends with children or invite other children to play.

- Teach simple chores that may be useful at nursery, such as packing away toys.
- Help your child to recognise his name. Even if he can't read or write yet, he may be able to recognise the first letter of his name or even the whole thing.

IF THERE IS A PROBLEM WITH YOUR NURSERY

Ofsted's guidance notes give you a clear idea of the type and level of service you should expect from a childcare provider, including nurseries and childminders. If you have any concerns about the level of care, in the first instance, where possible, you should speak to the childcare provider; at a nursery, you speak to the manager. Many issues can be resolved at an early stage in this way and may just be down to a misunderstanding.

If you are unable to speak directly to the manager about your concerns, feel uncomfortable to do so or that you have already had unsatisfactory contact with them about an issue, you can contact Ofsted's complaints line. Ofsted will investigate complaints and come back to you. They will follow up with appropriate action, right up to de-registering a service where quality is not meeting the national standards. If you have serious or urgent concerns about your child's safety, remove them from the nursery immediately and contact the child-protection team at your local Social Services. You should also contact the Ofsted complaints line to let them know what you have done.

WORKPLACE NURSERIES AND CRÈCHES

Workplace nurseries (and/or play schemes run during school holidays) may offer an affordable childcare option for employees. Payments towards the workplace nursery on behalf of employees (possibly as part of a salary-sacrifice scheme – see website and Appendix 2) are exempt from tax and National Insurance contributions, making a saving for the employee and the employer. However, due to the high cost involved, workplace nurseries are often restricted to larger organisations.

Many employers choose to work with existing nurseries by inviting them to tender for provision of a nursery on site. However, there is an alternative in the form of a workplace nursery partnership. Many providers believe that this type of scheme can offer more choice and flexibility than on-site nurseries.

Workplace nursery partnership schemes allow employers to select and register with government-approved nurseries across the country and, provided the company supports the nursery with finance or partly manages it, employees can still receive tax relief on the cost of using the facility. Through a workplace nursery partnership scheme, employees are able to take their children to a childcare facility near their home, then commute to work.

On-site nursery and childcare facilities mean parents don't have the hassle of a separate nursery run and are also nearby if a problem arises, but in a big city like London, parents may choose not to involve their child in an uncomfortable commute to work every day.

Goldman Sachs has found that its on-site emergency child-care has enabled staff to remain at work if they are let down by childcare arrangements. According to the results of a recent staff survey, 96 per cent of those using the back-up service agreed that it allowed them to stay in the office when they would otherwise have had to take time off. A certain number of places at its nursery are reserved each day for emergencies.

The nursery, which is open every weekday between 7 a.m. and 6.15 p.m., is available for children aged three months to eleven years. Each employee is allowed up to 20 days' care per child per year, and new mothers receive an extra 20 consecutive days on their return from maternity leave. This service is ranked among staff as among their most valued benefits. 'We benefit from reduced absenteeism, higher productivity and increased commitment . . . One of the most powerful benefits of the programme is the improved retention of our working mothers.'

CHILDREN'S CENTRES

Children's centres are a relatively recent government initiative, offering a combination of services and activities, including childcare for under-fives, healthcare, family support and help for parents looking for work. The childcare element usually takes the form of a day nursery, probably run privately; the other services on offer are accessible to everyone whether or not they are using the daycare facility. These centres are springing up all over the country, with the aim that by 2010 they will be available for all under-fives in every community.

Children's centres are a vital part of the government's 10-year childcare strategy to enable all families with children to have access to an affordable, flexible, high-quality childcare place. The aim is for children and their families to receive seamless integrated services and information, and access help from multi-disciplinary teams of professionals.

Each centre should provide the following services.

- Early learning integrated with full daycare, including early identification of, and provision for, children with special educational needs and disabilities.
- Outreach services to families in the area.
- Family support, including support for parents with special needs.
- Health services including antenatal care.
- A base for childminders and a service hub within the community for parents and providers of childcare services.
- Effective links with Jobcentre Plus, local training providers and further- and higher-education institutions.
- Effective links with children's information services, neighbourhood nurseries, out-of-school clubs and extended schools.
- Management and workforce training.

The concept isn't new. A significant number of families with young children already benefit from good-quality integrated services, and the new children's centres enhance these services and extend the benefits to more families in the community.

You may choose a children's centre as your childcare setting if:

- there is one local to you
- you like the idea of a one-stop shop providing integrated services, advice and support

- the social side appeals to you – connecting with other parents, carers and families
- your child or children is/are under five

POLICY AND IMPLEMENTATION

Local authorities have been given strategic responsibility for the delivery of children's centres. They are planning their location and development to meet the needs of local communities in consultation with parents, the private, voluntary and independent sector, PCTs, Jobcentre Plus and other key organisations. The government has contracted with a partnership of private- and public-sector organisations, called Together for Children, to provide delivery support on the ground for local authorities.

Until 2006 Sure Start children's centres were located where need was greatest – local authorities focused on children living in wards that were among the most disadvantaged in the country. They also had the flexibility to develop centres in pockets of disadvantage outside these most disadvantaged areas where similarly high levels of need existed. By 2008 Sure Start children's centre services were reaching all children under five and their families in the most disadvantaged areas, as well as many families outside these areas, with 2,500 in total. By 2010, the aim is for children's centre services to be reaching all children under five and their families in all areas, with 3,500 in total.

HOW TO FIND A CHILDREN'S CENTRE

Your local authority education department should be able to give you a list of children's centres, and you can search on the government's Childcare Link website for centres in your area, as you can with all forms of registered childcare.

CHILDREN WITH SPECIAL NEEDS

Your child's children's centre should be able to help your child overcome the barriers presented by their special needs, but it is possible that he or she will need extra support for some or all of their time in early-years education. (See Appendix 3, pages 301–3.)

THINGS TO CONSIDER

You will need to ask all of the usual questions (see page 211) when choosing a children's centre for your child with a few extras.

- Do the carers have experience in looking after a child with a similar disability? If not, would they be happy for you to show them what's needed?
- How much specialist care does your child need and is appropriate training available locally for nursery or children's-centre staff?
- Does your child have therapy or appointments she needs to go to during the time she will be cared for? If so, will your nursery take her to them?

- Does the carer need specialist training or equipment? Often carers have to have specific training to give medication. As a parent, you'll be shown how to give medication to your child by your doctor, nurse or health visitor. You can ask the same person to give this training to your child's new carer.

EARLY-YEARS SPECIAL EDUCATIONAL NEEDS CO-ORDINATORS (SENCOS)

Children's centres should all have a SENCo who will create opportunities for children with special needs to enjoy all the activities the centre offers.

Early-years area SENCos (sometimes called inclusion officers) give additional support to children's centres by offering training and specialist advice, and liaising with schools when the child is ready to go to full-time education.

Before your child starts, you should ask to meet the SENCo to talk about her and how the children's centre will be able to help. Ask to see their special educational needs policy and inclusion statement.

Once your child is in the children's centre, the SENCo will work with you to make sure that:

- your child's individual education plan (IEP) is written so that everybody knows how to help her (the SENCo should meet with you every term to review the IEP)
- extra advice and support is available if necessary
- everybody working with your child is kept up to date with her progress

- important information is collected, recorded and updated

There are three stages of help.

Early Years Action When your child is not learning some of the things other children do at the same age, staff make an IEP to help her progress. This lists the extra support and activities that will help her.

Early Years Action Plus If staff have done everything on the IEP and your child is still not progressing some months later, your nursery may decide to get extra advice. This may be from a speech and language therapist, a health visitor or other health service.

Statement of special educational needs This may be agreed after a statutory assessment of your child's needs has taken place. A statement can clarify your child's areas of difficulty and guide the nursery in using extra support and specialist programmes to meet her needs. As young children are still developing, it is usually better for the assessment to take place when she is a little older and assessment results are more reliable.

SUMMARY

Before deciding on a nursery or children's centre, have you considered:

- which is the most appropriate for you and your child?
- the cost implications?
- the results of Ofsted inspections?
- waiting lists?
- visiting local nurseries and children's centres to assess the provision and facilities of each setting?
- the age and disposition of your child?
- the hours the nursery is open?

A nursery should provide a safe, clean, happy and sociable childcare setting with opportunities for your child to engage in a wide variety of activities, year round, at moderate cost. Ofsted inspections, qualified staff and child–staff ratios offer many parents more reassurance than engaging an individual nanny to care for their baby. However, with more than one child at nursery, even with the sibling discount that most nurseries offer, cost may become an issue, and the practicalities of combining nursery care with school runs may be a good reason to look at other options.

CHAPTER 9

Nursery Schools, Playgroups and School-based Care

NURSERY SCHOOLS

A nursery school generally offers part-time education and care for children aged between two and a half (or three in some cases) and five (or older in some private nursery schools). It may exist independently or as a department within a junior or primary school. It will be staffed by trained teachers, nursery nurses and classroom assistants. Private nursery schools are sometimes called nurseries, or preschools, or even kindergartens, which may confuse the issue, but they all do more or less the same thing.

Nursery schools do not generally offer full-time daycare, but see School-based Care, page 239. A nursery school has to be registered with the government regulatory bodies and is inspected every year. It will offer a government-approved early-years curriculum, following the Early Years Foundation Stage (EYFS) framework, which sets the standards for learning, development and care of children from birth to five. The EYFS replaced the variety of previous frameworks that included the non-statutory Birth to Three Matters, and the National Standards for Under Eights Day Care and Childminding. All registered early-years providers and schools were required to use the EYFS from September 2008.

AGES COVERED AND STAFF RATIO

Nursery schools and classes cater for preschool children from three to five. The child–staff ratio for children in a nursery school is 20–26 children to two adults, where one of those adults is a qualified teacher and the other is a trained nursery nurse or classroom assistant.

A nursery school may be the right option for you if:

- your child is between three and five (although some private nursery schools offer sessional care for younger children)
- you don't work, or can work within the nursery-school hours
- you work but your nanny, childminder or other carer can incorporate nursery school into the daily routine
- you want to give your child the opportunity to enjoy this transitional phase between home and school

TIMETABLE

Most nursery schools and classes operate during school hours (9 a.m. to 3.30 p.m.), with normal school holidays of around 13 weeks per year. Most offer five half-day sessions, although some will offer part- or full-time places.

PROS

- A nursery school or class will be registered and regularly inspected.
- Your child will be taught by qualified staff.
- There will be a structured learning programme, appropriate to age.
- The children will learn in age-based groups.
- They may have contact with older, school-age children.
- If the nursery school is not part of a school, your child may be able to move directly to a linked school.

CONS

- You may need additional childcare.
- A nursery school will not care for a sick child.
- You may have to live within the catchment area for a particular school's nursery department.
- There may be a waiting list for your chosen nursery school.
- Fees may be payable, although your child may be entitled to a free part-time place – see website for details.
- The ratios of children to carers are much higher than in most other childcare settings.
- Your child may find five half-day sessions very tiring.
- There is less parental interaction with a nursery school than with a playgroup.
- A place at a nursery school does not guarantee a place in the reception class that follows.

TYPICAL COSTS

State nursery schools are free, but private nursery schools may charge around £1,000 a term. However, fees vary widely and depend on where you live. Current legislation provides every three- and four-year-old in England with 12.5 hours of free early-learning per week, in nursery schools, playgroups, preschools or at their childminder's for 38 weeks of the year. From 2010, this will rise to 15 hours per week, delivered flexibly over a minimum of three days. See Appendix 2, page 297.

The table that follows shows when your child will become eligible for their free early-learning place.

IF YOUR CHILD IS BORN BETWEEN:	THEY ARE ELIGIBLE FOR A FREE PLACE FROM:
1 April and 31 August	1 September following their third birthday until statutory school age
1 September and 31 December	1 January following their third birthday until statutory school age
1 January and 31 March	1 April following their third birthday until statutory school age

If the free entitlement doesn't cover your family's needs – for example, because of work commitments – you may be able to get financial help with the cost of extra childcare. See the website for details.

Although there's no guarantee that you will be offered a place with a particular provider, your local authority should be able to give you a list of registered providers and will take your preference into account wherever possible.

CHOOSING A NURSERY SCHOOL

Nursery schools are registered and inspected by Ofsted. Many providers of early education are also accredited through a quality assurance (QA) scheme that will only accredit providers if they meet certain standards, and are committed to keeping those standards by monitoring their work. You can ask for a copy of the latest Ofsted report and always ask if a nursery school belongs to a QA scheme. Talk to other parents and find out what the grapevine says about local nursery schools – you will glean a lot of information that's hard to come by elsewhere.

Nursery provision within schools for children aged three and over is not required to be registered because it is already taken into account by the main school-inspection framework. It is, however, expected to meet the same standards as other providers. All settings are regularly inspected against EYFS requirements.

You may want to ask the nursery school about:

- opening times and holiday dates
- charges (if any)
- healthy meals and special diets
- emergency procedures
- policies on child protection
- the ratio of children to staff
- the range of activities and resources
- how any additional and special educational needs will be met
- how you get to know about and involved in your child's learning and progress

- how children are involved in the planning of activities
- whether there is provision for staff to continue to learn about children and their needs
- what happens when your child is sick
- whether your child will meet the same children and adults every time they attend
- whether staff are qualified and experienced
- whether staff are aware of confidentiality and privacy
- whether staff work in partnership with parents

When you visit the nursery school, try to ascertain:

- whether children are calm, safe, happy and playing together
- whether staff are friendly and welcoming
- whether staff are listening, talking and interacting appropriately with children
- whether staff are managing behaviour appropriately
- whether the setting is safe, clean and secure
- whether the setting is welcoming and stimulating
- whether there is outdoor space
- whether there are places where children can rest

WHAT TO EXPECT FROM A NURSERY SCHOOL

Between the ages of three and five, children follow the EYFS curriculum, which is designed to provide opportunities for all children to succeed in an atmosphere of care and to feel valued. It prepares them for all future learning by supporting, fostering, promoting and developing them, and is divided into six areas of learning.

Personal, social and emotional development To help your child learn to be self-confident, take an interest in things, know what their own needs are, tell the difference between right and wrong, and be able to dress and undress.

Communication, language and literacy To help children learn to talk confidently and clearly, enjoy stories, songs and poems, hear and say sounds, and link them to the alphabet. They will read and write some familiar words and learn to use a pencil.

Mathematical development Your child will develop an understanding of maths through stories, songs, games and imaginative play. He will become comfortable with numbers and with ideas such as 'heavier than' or 'bigger'. He will be aware of shapes and space.

Knowledge and understanding of the world Your child will explore and find out about the world around him, asking questions. He will build with different materials, know about everyday technology and learn what it is used for. He will find out about past events in his and his family's lives, different cultures and beliefs.

Physical development Your child will learn to move confidently, controlling his body and handling equipment.

Creative development Your child will explore colours and shapes, trying out dance, making things and music, and telling stories. The early-learning goals set out the skills, understanding, knowledge and attitudes it is hoped children will reach or exceed by the end of the EYFS. An integral part of the EYFS is play, both adult-led and child-initiated, indoors and out, as this is a key way in which young children learn. Sometimes they will choose what they want to do. At other times they take part in activities that help them learn how to concentrate or develop a particular skill, like using scissors or gluing card.

YOUR CHILD'S PROGRESS

An assessment based on observations by teachers of children in everyday activities is made at the end of the EYFS called the Foundation Stage Profile. This is a national scheme that enables teachers to record observations and summarise your child's achievements. It shows how well your child has progressed with the early-learning goals and covers all six areas of learning. At the end of the EYFS you will receive a folder recording his progress, including art and written work, 'real-time' observations – 'Thomas is trying to do a puzzle, and he has just thrown it on the floor' – a record of when various milestones have been reached, such as going to the toilet alone, sitting nicely on the carpet, and the odd photograph. It is a classic piece of childhood memorabilia that will bring your family (or has brought mine) plenty of amusement.

PREPARING YOUR CHILD FOR NURSERY SCHOOL

Your child may be anxious about what to expect on the first day at nursery school. If so, talk through his fears: explain where he will be going, what he'll be doing, and for how long; answer questions, and iron out any anxiety by asking what he thinks it may be like; emphasise the things he may enjoy doing. Don't dismiss his fears: things that seem obvious or silly to an adult can seem like terrible obstacles to a five-year-old.

If children have a good idea of what school will be like and have already experienced learning activities at home and in other settings, they're less likely to find the experience stressful. Games, role-plays and reading at home can help your child get into the right frame of mind and boost their confidence. For example:

- playing games that involve taking turns or speaking in front of a group
- playing with children of a similar age to develop social skills
- reading books about starting school
- using your child's favourite toys to role-play going to school
- painting and drawing, which involve sitting down for short periods of time

You could also help him prepare for the new setting if you:

- involve him in choosing things he needs for nursery school, such as a school bag or uniform
- visit the nursery school with your child so he becomes familiar with the building and the local area
- establish a routine and discuss what might be happening at nursery school at different times of the day

PLAYGROUPS

Playgroups provide an important transition phase before a child enters full-time education. A playgroup offers sessional care, and parents or carers will drop off the children and collect them at the end of the session. It will be Ofsted-registered, will follow the EYFS framework and monitor your child's development, providing a structured, stimulating learning environment.

SIMILARITIES AND DIFFERENCES BETWEEN PLAYGROUPS AND NURSERY SCHOOLS

Both nursery schools and playgroups provide an important transition phase before a child enters full-time education. Both provide sessional care, and parents or carers will drop off their children and collect them at the end of the session. Both nursery schools and playgroups will be Ofsted-registered, follow the EYFS framework and will monitor your child's development. Both will provide a structured, stimulating learning environment for children.

There are also a number of essential differences between the two.

Nursery School	Playgroup
Over threes	Usually available from two and a half
Based in a primary or junior school or feeding into one	Usually based in a community centre or church hall

Usually three-hour sessions Start with or build up to a five-day week Parents not expected to help or run the school Around £1,000 a term (private) or free in state system	Usually two-and-a-half-hour sessions Start with or build up to three or four sessions You may be expected to get involved on a rota system Up to £5 a session

Playgroups should be distinguished from parent-and-toddler groups, which operate effectively as drop-in centres where parents, nannies and childminders get together with their children and charges for a mixture of free play and some organised activities such as Play-Doh and arts and crafts.

AGES COVERED

Playgroups usually accept children from two and a half, or whenever they are out of nappies. Typically, your child might attend a playgroup for a year before she starts nursery school.

ESSENTIAL ADVANTAGES OF PLAYGROUPS

- They are community-based.
- Your child will be among others of her own age.
- Your child will have access to excellent play and learning opportunities.

- You should be able to become involved.
- It's a great way to meet other parents.
- It makes for an easy transition to nursery school.

SCHOOL-BASED CARE

For parents of school-age children, childcare has always been particularly problematic. Few private day nurseries will do school or nursery-school drop-offs, and nannies prepared to do before- and after-school care are an expensive option, as well as a bit thin on the ground. In response to this, as well as (primarily) with the aim of lifting children out of poverty and improving their chances in life, the government set up the extended-schools programme. The idea is that schools not only stay open from 8 a.m. till 6 p.m. but offer a range of services including childcare, study support, sport and music clubs, parenting and family support, and access to relevant specialist services. The school works in partnership with other agencies that have an interest in outcomes for children and young people, and with the local community. All school-based childcare is registered and inspected by Ofsted.

TYPES OF SCHOOL-BASED CARE

The childcare element of the extended school can be divided roughly into four parts: breakfast clubs, after-school clubs, wraparound care and holiday play schemes.

Breakfast clubs A breakfast club is a place where children can be dropped off before school (around 8 a.m.) and enjoy breakfast together in a supervised setting. Some clubs offer activities that support learning at school, and statistics show that they even improve performance in the classroom. Your child's school or your local authority will have more information on breakfast clubs she can attend – although most will be located in primary schools.

After-school clubs An after-school club, or homework club, is a place for children to go after the school day has finished but office hours haven't, usually from around 3.30 p.m. to 6 p.m. Children can do homework or join in games or sports, art and craft. The club may be in your child's school, another local school or different premises altogether. Play-workers will usually escort children to and from the school and the club.

Wraparound care This is a new concept in school-based care, allowing children as young as three, who are at nursery-school stage, to stay at school for the whole day. If your child has a place at the afternoon nursery session at the local primary school, you can drop her off at 9 a.m. (usually with a packed lunch) and she will have a full school day rather than just the three hours in the afternoon. These wraparound arrangements usually cater for part-time care as well, so part-days may be available. If your local primary school doesn't offer this service, it may be part of a local cluster of schools that offer this service at the school that has space and facilities. The wraparound service should include accompanying your child to and from his school to the wraparound-care centre. You may like to combine wraparound care with a childminder or nanny. It won't suit the average working parent, though, as it won't usually stay open till 6 p.m.

because after-school clubs are designed for school-age (4+) only. Sally says:

> *I run my own business from home, and can get away with working only during school hours. When my older boy started school, I still had the little one at nursery, at the same school, and needed to find cover between nursery and school finish times. It was then that the school set up wraparound care. A local nursery effectively moved into the classroom that was used for breakfast club and after-school care, and looked after nursery children during the rest of the school hours. I just had to bring him in at 9 a.m. with a packed lunch and water bottle and they did the rest. I was particularly lucky that it was at our school that the care was based – children at other primary-school nurseries within the school cluster had to be walked some distance every day to and from the wraparound centre. It was a fantastic service, staffed by lovely and dedicated nursery nurses, and they had use of the school playground facilities as well. It was great value for money, my boys could stay together and I could work from home without having a nanny or au pair under my feet. Wrap-around care effectively saved my business and came in just at the right time.*

Holiday play schemes Play schemes operate in the school holidays and offer groups of children a range of organised activities, from art and craft to outings. They are usually open between 8.30 a.m. and 6 p.m. and will be based at a local school. Costs vary but the state-run play schemes that operate within primary schools are generally less than half the price of some private holiday camps. When it comes down to it, though, most children are happy to go wherever their friends are going. Some private nurseries and nursery schools also offer holiday care.

THE BENEFITS OF EXTENDED SCHOOLS

Research shows that extended services can have significant positive effects on children, parents, families and schools. Pupil-attainment rates increase and exclusions drop. An Ofsted evaluation in 2006 suggested that extended services are also helping to enhance self-confidence, improve relationships, raise aspirations and produce better attitudes to learning.

The extended opening hours mean that parents now have greater choice, flexibility, convenience and accessibility to help them balance family and work commitments. Working parents on lower incomes, who are accessing childcare through their school, can benefit from claiming the childcare element of the working tax credit, which can cover up to 80 per cent of the costs.

See Appendix 2, page 297.

WORKING IN PARTNERSHIP

Many schools will choose to work in partnership with existing local private and voluntary-sector providers, or by building on existing links with other local schools and working as a cluster.

The provision of quick and easy access to services such as health and social care means that problems affecting children's learning can be more rapidly dealt with. Where families are engaged in activities such as family learning, they become more involved in their children's education, embrace new learning opportunities and encourage their children to learn.

PROS

- An after-school club, breakfast club or play scheme that caters for under-eights for more than two hours a day will be registered and regularly inspected.
- If it's registered, it will be run by approved play-workers, half of whom will be qualified.
- The setting will be familiar to your child.
- It is likely to be local or easily accessible.
- It can bridge those awkward gaps between school and work hours.
- Your child will be among a group of other children, some younger, some older.
- Your child will have access to a variety of play opportunities.
- You may be able to opt for a regular part-time place, which will offer her consistency.

CONS

- Some out-of-school services – for example, those that cater for over-eights only or operate for less than two hours a day – won't be registered, but many of these are quality assured (QA), a government-recognised scheme, so always check whether the one you're using is registered or QA and, if it isn't, make sure you're satisfied with the care provided.

- After-school clubs can be very busy and your child may prefer to relax at home.
- Out-of-school care may be a bit overwhelming for a younger or shy child.
- If your child is attending an after-school club every day, it can be hard for her to have time on her own, meet her friends or follow her own particular interests.
- The staff won't be able to look after your child if she's ill.
- Fees may be payable.

TYPICAL COSTS

Fees vary widely across the country, from around £3–10 a day for an after-school-club place; and around £15 a day, or £75 a week, for a play-scheme place.

CHILDREN WITH SPECIAL NEEDS

Your child's nursery school or playgroup should be able to help your child overcome the barriers presented by their special needs, but it is possible that he will need extra support.

Bear in mind that:

- your child's needs will usually be met in a playgroup or nursery school, sometimes with the help of outside specialists
- you should be asked about the decisions that affect your child
- your views should always be taken into account

THINGS TO CONSIDER

You will need to ask all of the usual questions when choosing a nursery school, playgroup or school-based care for your child, with a few extras.

- Do the carers have experience in looking after a child with a similar disability? If not, would they be happy for you to show them what's needed?
- How much specialist care does your child need and is appropriate training available locally?
- Does your child have therapy or appointments that she needs to go to during the time she will be cared for and can your nursery school, playgroup or school-based care facility take her to them?
- Does the carer need specialist training or equipment? Often carers have to have specific training to give medication. As a parent, you'll be shown how to give medication to your child by your doctor, nurse or health visitor. You can ask the same person to give this training to your child's new carer.

See also page 225 for information on early-years special educational needs co-ordinators (SENCos).

SUMMARY

If your child is preschool, have you considered the option of school-based nursery care as opposed to a private nursery school, and have you:

- considered the cost implications?
- visited the available settings to view the provision and facilities and meet teachers?
- seen the results of Ofsted inspections?
- asked about waiting lists and selection criteria?
- considered whether you will need to take advantage of wraparound care?
- asked the opinions of other local parents?
- taken into account the nature and disposition of your child?
- thought about combining this with a childminder or nanny, if required, the costs and practicalities of that?

If your child is ready for school, have you considered whether or not you will need to take advantage of breakfast clubs, after-school clubs and holiday clubs? In particular have you looked at:

- whether the care is based at your school or another school?
- the convenience of the location?
- the provision and facilities?
- the practicality and waiting lists?
- extra-curricular activities?
- combining this with using a childminder or nanny, if required, the costs and practicalities of that?

Nursery schools and playgroups provide an essential introduction to education, yet the huge choice available can make the whole decision seem pretty daunting. For many, the simple matter of cost will enable them to rule out private nursery-school care, but if you have the option of paying, you will have more thinking to do. Most parents say that the recommendation of other parents drove them to make the key decisions at this point, and gut instinct on looking around the setting in question. You know your child better than anyone and are likely to have a good idea of which variety of preschool education would be most appropriate.

CHAPTER 10

Using Relatives

A recent study by the Department for Education and Skills (DFES) shows that around half of all families use informal child-care arrangements. Despite the creation of half a million new nursery places and a pledge from the government of affordable childcare for all, the number of families turning to grandparents, aunts and even neighbours appears to be on the increase.

The study found that the percentage of families using formal childcare had fallen from 57 per cent to 54 per cent in the past three years, the prime reason being affordability and cost: 'Despite a small improvement in parents' views on the affordability of childcare, cost remains an important barrier to the use of childcare for some parents, especially large families and those with younger children.'

It is not surprising then that more people are relying on relatives to look after their children – and they seem to be making a good choice: research shows that children actually grow up happier if their grandparents are involved in their upbringing. A recent survey by the Centre for Research into Parenting and Children in the Department of Social Policy and Social Work at Oxford University recently questioned more than 1,500 children and teenagers who had been cared for by grandparents. The survey revealed a huge amount of informal caring by grandparents, who in some cases were filling the parental gap for hardworking parents; and also indicated a strong link between involved grandparents and adolescent well-being.

In theory, you could ask any competent and capable relative to look after your children. Since these are usually informal arrangements, there are no statistics to show how many people use which particular relation, but the most common choices are:

- grandparents – most common choice
- aunts/uncles – less common
- other children – if you have much older children or children from a previous relationship

Using relatives as childcarers may be a good option for you if:

- you have a competent and keen relative ready to do it
- cost is an issue and care is being offered free or for minimal pay
- your relative is local to you
- there is a suitable venue – either their place or yours
- he/she is fit and healthy
- he/she doesn't have and isn't likely to make any conflicting commitments
- you share the same childcare ethos

- you communicate well generally
- he/she wants the job on a commercial basis

COSTS

Although you're dealing with a family member, you may still want to agree an informal (or, indeed, formal) contract about hours, holidays, time off and whether or not you make any payment. See section on Remuneration, page 256.

PROS

- A family member, particularly a grandparent, is likely to love your child almost as much as you do.
- Your child will probably develop a close bond with the relative, which will enrich both their lives.
- A grandparent – or an aunt or uncle who is a parent – will be experienced with children.
- They may be more flexible about hours than a formal childcare arrangement.
- They may be prepared to drop off and collect from nursery or school.
- They may be able to look after your child if she's sick.
- Your child may be able to have friends round to play.
- Your child will be cared for in a familiar environment.
- Your child will have continuity of care.
- Less settling-in will be required.

CONS

- A relative, particularly an older one, may find the physical demands of a young child exhausting, however willing they are.
- Any existing tension between you may be exacerbated.
- There may be strings attached: if you use their help for free, then take an expensive holiday, there may be questions to answer . . .
- They may have pre-existing commitments and interests.
- Granny may be in the habit of spoiling her grandchildren – and may find it hard to break.
- They may want to take more holiday than is convenient for you.
- Coming from a different generation, they may have a different childcare ethos.
- You may want your child to meet other young children, but an older relative may not feel comfortable attending a playgroup predominantly for young mothers.
- Informal arrangements can go wrong, and if they do, it's your own family you're falling out with – potentially causing a long-term rift.

MAKING RELATIVE CARE WORK

Most parents and relatives begin care arrangements with high hopes and warm feelings all round. But relative care can also complicate your relationship in unexpected ways. You are no longer just mother and daughter, or mother and daughter-in-law, but also parent and childcarer. Grandparents, although often keen and capable childcarers, have their own needs, which they may feel are sometimes overlooked. Unlike other employees, they will not want to raise a grievance, and small niggles can easily escalate into a breakdown in the relationship. The website www.grannynet.co.uk is like an online support group for grandparents and has established a Grandparents' Charter, a set of guidelines 'for grandparents and parents to refer to when embarking on any childcare arrangement to make it work successfully for both parties'. Here are some top tips for making it work.

Do your homework Before you engage your maiden aunt or great-grandfather to be the primary carer for your child, make sure you have addressed the key issues of whether she or he is really right for the job. You won't want to put them through a formal interview process, but you should go through some sort of assessment process in your head to check that your candidate, regardless of family membership, is up to it.

- The *ability* of the relative to provide the childcare is the most important consideration. He or she must be physically and emotionally fit and, in the case of a grandparent, this may be the greatest obstacle to making the decision. As women wait longer and longer to have children, so the pool of grandparents caring for children is ageing, and the issues of both physical and mental health must be addressed. Sit down with your relative and discuss the demands of the job honestly – not just the physical work involved but the emotional pressure of dealing with tantrums, puberty and other aspects of child development.

- Personality: will he or she provide a nurturing environment for your child? Will they be patient with him or her? Just as significant is their ability to accept suggestions from you – will they take offence if you ask them to handle a parenting issue in a different way from the one they are used to?
- Transport: do you need Granny to drive your car? Is she a safe driver? You will need to make sure she is aware of all the legislation on car and booster seats and how to install them properly.
- Be sure the offer of care is genuine and not made out of politeness or a sense of obligation.
- Has Granny momentarily forgotten about her bridge afternoon on Thursdays and their cruise to Madeira next week?
- Are they sufficiently local – or if not local, is the journey manageable in the rush-hour, and do they appreciate how crucial punctuality is to you?
- How happy is Granny to stay an extra hour now and then when you are running late? It is no bargain if the parents often find themselves having to find back-up care because the relative has other demands on their time. You may feel you can't complain because of the deal you are getting on childcare, leading to resentment and strain on the family relationship.
- Is this a stop-gap or is your relative in it for the long-haul?

Get a written agreement Whether you are at the planning stage or have already begun, make sure you have a written agreement between you, setting out all your arrangements clearly, just as you would for a nanny or childminder, but taking into account the nature of your existing relationship. Here are some essential clauses for your agreement:

(a) amount you will pay, and when
(b) holiday – how much, when it is to be taken (in most arrangements, parents choose half and nannies – or grannies – choose the other half)
(c) snacks and meals: what your child will eat, when and who will provide it
(d) daily schedule, including indoor and outdoor play, nap times, special activities and rules about use of television, DVDs, computers and electronic games
(e) behaviour and discipline
(f) health and safety – perhaps you can ask him or her to help you childproof your home and theirs
(g) emergency information:

- name, address and phone number for you and/or your spouse at work
- name, address and phone number of other emergency contacts
- name, address and phone number of your child's doctor
- information on your child's special health issues, allergies or medication
- written consent for emergency medical treatment if you cannot be reached

Establish the ground rules You want to be sure (without being patronising, of course) that your relative takes the childcare role seriously. The first step to achieving that is being clear about everything you want and expect, at the same time as acknowledging that Granny might want to post a letter or do her ironing. Think about what sort of errands you are happy for her to take your child on, how much time she will spend cooking or cleaning while your child is there. If you can talk about these concerns before they become problems you might save yourself a lot of difficult conversations at a later stage.

Communicate – and listen! Whether your child is being cared for by a nanny, a childminder or Granny, it's always a good idea to talk about how the day went. Try to have a thorough discussion once a week, to make sure things are going smoothly, to express your appreciation and to listen to feedback, including any reservations she may have. It can be much harder for a relative to address some issues than a formally sourced childcarer. Make sure the discussion is two-way. Granny has brought up at least one child (presumably) and although you may consider some of her instinctive methods old-fashioned, she may have valuable advice to impart, and showing her you are ready to listen to (but not necessarily follow) that advice will help build trust between you.

Remuneration Everyone has different arrangements for rewarding a relative for their childcare role. Some grandparents won't take a penny for it and see it as a privilege and an honour (although we had trouble locating anyone to give us a quote to that effect) and others are happy to take a fair salary. What you pay Granny or your sister-in-law may range from nothing, or just expenses, to a full commercial rate.

If you cannot afford to pay her, think about whether there is anything you can offer in exchange for her services – transport, errands, etc.

Tax breaks using Granny You can't usually claim tax credits for childcare provided by relatives, even if they are registered or approved. If Granny (for the sake of argument) does the childcare in her own home, you can save money by getting her to register as a childminder, thereby entitling you to benefit from the voucher and salary-sacrifice schemes (see Appendix 2, pages 293–7). However, if she goes down this route, and you are to qualify for these tax savings, she will have to look after other children as well as yours. To sum up: if childcare is provided in your home by a relative, you will not benefit from the voucher scheme – and a relative is defined, whether by blood, half-blood, marriage or civil partnership, as a:

- parent
- step-parent
- foster-parent
- grandparent
- aunt or uncle
- brother or sister

Childcare provided by a relative may qualify for the purposes of vouchers if:

- the relative is a 'registered' or 'approved' childcare provider;
- the care is provided away from the child's own home; and
- the care is provided to non-related children in addition to the related child or children.

Help with information and support As we all know, taking care of children is hard work and anyone in the job can sometimes feel isolated, or may not have all the resources or skills they need. Granny may feel more confident if she has taken a first-aid course – if you can help her find one, pay for it, or even go on the course together, you will both feel better equipped. Introduce her to other mothers, carers, nannies or childminders as appropriate, and take her to local parent-and-toddler groups so that she is familiar with the route, the set-up and procedure – a lot may have changed since she had children of that age.

PERSONAL FAMILY ISSUES

Another potential sticking point that you may not have thought of is the possibility of family conflicts boiling over with the childcare arrangement. Discord may result directly from relative care, such as a disagreement over a parenting issue. A different possibility, however, is that some prior source of strife between you and the care-giving relative is aggravated because of the new relationship you share. For example, if you feel that your mother was always less than responsive to your worries and problems when you were a child, you may become upset with her if you perceive her as distant towards your own children. If you feel that your mother-in-law is overbearing or bossy to you and your spouse, it may make you bristle to hear her dole out orders to your children, even if it would be perfectly acceptable to you when a babysitter did exactly the same thing.

MAINTAINING GOOD 'RELATIONS'

If Granny doesn't seem up to the job, or if you have any concerns about the way things are or aren't working out, you may feel more uncomfortable addressing the issue than you would with a nanny or childminder. The nature of your relationship means that any parting of the ways that may occur as a result of a disagreement will have quite a marked effect on family relations. A rift in a mother–daughter relationship may be easier to repair than in a mother–daughter-in-law relationship, the usual rule being that 'My mum just isn't up to it' is much easier to say to your husband than 'Your mum just isn't up to it.' It may also be easier to approach your own parent to discuss their childcare techniques than your partner's parent, and therefore for your partner to make the first approach if the problem lies in that direction. Nevertheless, the success of the whole Granny-as-nanny scenario rests on finding diplomatic solutions to any difficulties that arise. Here are my top tips for avoiding upsets when using a relative as your childcarer.

Choose your battles Decide what is really important, and be flexible about other things. For instance, if Granny is being impatient about toilet training and generally a bit too strict, you might decide to talk first about how – and when – she plans to begin toilet training, then wait a week before discussing rules and children's behaviour.

Describe your concerns from the child's viewpoint Instead of saying, 'I don't like what you're doing,' say, 'Toby is so active, I think he needs to play outside more often.' Or, 'At her check-up,

Laura's doctor suggested we get her together more with other children.'

Find a good time to talk It is important for children to know that you like and trust the relative who cares for them, so don't discuss problems when the children are around. This goes for any form of childcare.

Express your affection and approval even when you disagree Bringing up a problem may be harder with a relative than with a non-relative, but it can also be easier because you have shared history and shared love for your children. Calling on earlier good times or memories can help you solve the problem.

In the midst of all this tact and diplomacy, remember that your wishes should not be ignored, even if your relative does not agree with you. If you have talked it over, and he or she continues to ignore your suggestions, you might have to take the drastic step of making other arrangements.

IS IT TIME FOR A CHANGE?

For many families, relative childcare feels right and works perfectly, but others will run into problems from time to time.

Here are the most common reported problems with using relatives for childcare.

- ➤ You get unwanted advice every day about how the children should eat/play, etc.

- General family friction spills over into the childcare situation, which then becomes a source of stress rather than support.
- Children grow and their needs change: care that was perfect for your little one may seem less appropriate for an older child; you may find that your ageing parents can no longer keep up with active young children.
- The birth of another baby overwhelms even the most devoted grandparents.
- The relative or their spouse becomes ill.
- It becomes necessary to drive a car to take children to school and the relative is a non-driver.
- Discipline issues: Granny is too strict or too lenient. It can be a case of leopards and spots here, and differences of opinion on what is and isn't naughty or punishable may sometimes be impossible to resolve.
- Granny is suddenly the favourite carer and the children prefer to be looked after by her than by their parents.

Here is Heather's story:

> *My brother has been my children's nanny for over a year now. The situation came about when he was working part-time as a writer from home and was basically looking for the extra cash. He doesn't have children of his own and he and his wife love spending time with their nieces and nephew. We started with just the odd afternoon when I had a meeting that meant I couldn't do the school pick-up. Then when I set up my business I began to need a lot more help, so three hours a week soon developed into more like twenty, with my*

requirements being different every week, and even every day. I was so lucky he had that flexibility. He was happy to babysit, drive the kids to activities, look after the playdates and help with homework. He's even a very good cook and the whole thing is great for the children, who look forward to him coming. It's lovely that they have a male influence as well, with all the women in their lives – Mummy, teachers, other people's mummies . . . and I know it's a bit sexist to say this but I think he has toughened the girls up a bit. I can quite understand why people choose to have male nannies. I think they provide a real balance to the female overload children get these days.

SUMMARY

If you are thinking of using a relative as childcare, have you considered all the pros and cons above, and have you explored other forms of care as well? If you are choosing a relative, make sure that he or she is completely happy with the arrangement – if they pull out prematurely you will have not only the practical inconvenience but potentially a family conflict as well. Explore all the ramifications with your partner, and listen to the views of your children if they are old enough. Take plenty of time to think and talk about it. Using relatives may sound idyllic but it is likely to be the most complicated childcare arrangement to terminate if things go wrong.

CHAPTER 11

From the Horse's Mouth: Parents' Experiences and Top Tips

The stories below are just a selection from the hundreds of parents who wanted to share their experiences. Each family has described their first foray into the world of childcare and listed their top tips for other parents.

Josie lives in Surrey with her four children, now aged between three and twelve.

> *We looked at childminders first (as it was so much cheaper) but the hours didn't fit – they tend to stop at 6 p.m., as do daycare nurseries, and I needed someone to care for the baby until 7 p.m. when I got home from work. Also, childminders and nurseries didn't work in cases of child illness and holidays weren't flexible. A nannyshare was cheaper than having an exclusive nanny but had all the benefits.*
>
> *My first nanny was absolutely fantastic and stayed for six and a half years until I was pregnant with my third child and*

I had to let her go. Coincidentally she became pregnant at the same time and didn't need to return to work. She is now a family friend. We shared her for the first two years with another family who had six-year-old twin girls. Then I had a second child and the other family got an au pair and didn't need a nanny any more. I then shared with a friend who had a baby the same age as my second child. She had another child after three years and gave up work, so I then had the nanny exclusively for a year.

The good aspect of the nannyshare was that it was less expensive than having a nanny to myself. The downside was that I had to fit in with the other family's holidays, and, in the first share, had to take my child to the other family's house.

I went back to work full-time after having my third child and only interviewed one nanny. She has also been very good and has been with me for five years. When I became pregnant with my fourth child and didn't need a nanny over the period of my maternity leave, she took temporary jobs for eight months so that she could return to me when I went back to work again, which I much appreciated.

Top tips:

- Be relaxed – I'm glad I've only had two nannies over twelve years, which has given continuity for the children. I gather that this is quite unusual. My second nanny's temporary jobs included working for a woman who instructed her on how to boil pasta and had her cleaning the piano keys with a toothbrush. This woman (whose daughter goes to school with mine) has got through hordes of nannies and au pairs.

- I would say that one reason my nannies stayed with me is that I don't interfere. As long as the children are happy and the nanny is reliable then I am happy. I don't give instructions on what the children should eat or the activities they should do. On the other hand, I would also say that I have been extremely lucky with my two nannies and they didn't take advantage of my easy-going nature. They were just good professionals.

Gill has twins now aged ten, but first went back to work when they were six months old.

> *We decided to get a nanny mainly because the babies were twins and it was easier and cheaper to find childcare in the home. On top of that, my partner's sister had offered to be our nanny!*
>
> *The auntie solution was perfect for us. We paid her the going rate and she stayed for 18 months before emigrating to Australia. She hadn't had children herself so we basically trained her and she seemed to have no problem taking it all on board. I would have her back any day.*
>
> *We got our second nanny when the kids were two. I joined forces with my jobshare and when we heard that a nanny was not happy in her current situation we approached her and shared her. She was brilliant.*
>
> *It's very hard finding someone you can trust with your most important asset. We interviewed the nanny about her views on childcare and watched her interact with the children. We were really pleased with what we saw and didn't feel we needed to look any further. She stayed with us*

for four years, and I haven't a bad word to say about her. She planned things every day so I always came home to jam tarts, fruit flans, artwork of various shapes and sizes. The only issue arose when I became obsessed with my own timekeeping and would give her 15 minutes off on another day if I was late. In the end she told me off and I had to agree some ground rules. She was particularly good with the transition to school and did other chores for me during their nursery phase, which worked well.

Top tips:

- Be clear about what is important in the nanny.
- Use references and tailored questions to get the right information – don't look for all the good points because you want to like them.

The Andrews family live in central London and have two children now aged six and four.

The children have both been at full-time nursery since they were six months old, which was when we returned to full-time work. I used to live very close to the nursery in question and was aware of it before I had children. More importantly, a friend of mine had a son there and she was very happy with it. We didn't go to an agency and we didn't really look at other nurseries because this one seemed good and we had a personal recommendation. There was no problem settling my son at nursery and, once he started, I never had any doubt that he was being well looked after.

My first experience was of slight disappointment at how

pleased my son was to arrive at nursery each morning. Other children would wail when their parents left but Calum seemed only too pleased to see the back of me. The downside of nursery care is that you have the hassle of getting your child there and back. Also, they can't go if they're ill, and they don't get the one-to-one attention they would have with a nanny. But I took the view that this was more than compensated for by the interaction with other children and the activities on offer – I wasn't about to start making jam with my three-year-old at home. Plus I didn't have to rely on my own (wholly inexperienced) judgement in choosing an individual childcarer. I felt more comfortable putting the recruitment process in the hands of a professional nursery and trusting to a management system and the eyes of several members of staff rather than an individual who might or might not have been up to the job.

Top tips:

- It's boring but you should do the research and – if you're in London – do it *really* early as places get booked up fast. I applied while I was still pregnant and the nursery was not immediately able to promise me a place.
- Personal recommendation is best. If you don't know anyone in the area, you could try asking your health visitor or GP as they usually have an idea about local provision. Other than that, you have to visit a few different places and go by your instinct as to the feel and atmosphere of the nursery. Once you find one that seems like a possibility, you can ask to be introduced to some of the current parents to hear what they have to say.

- You can look at the Ofsted reports but I don't find them very enlightening or even an accurate reflection.
- Do what you feel comfortable with, and ignore anyone who tries to persuade you that their way is better.

The Hamiltons have two children, now aged one and three, and live in Manchester.

> *I use a Montessori nursery and the children joined when they were six months old. They attend four full days, from 8 a.m. to 6 p.m. It seemed the ideal choice as it was situated within walking distance of our home and was brand new. We didn't consider any other form of childcare because I decided I preferred a nursery environment over any other option.*
>
> *The nursery was opened a month after I returned to work with my first child so Darcy was the first baby to attend – and in fact was the only child to attend the nursery in its first week. The normal ratio of carer to child is one to three, but in this case the ratio was reversed and Darcy had three carers looking after her.*

Top tips:

- Go with your gut instinct about a nursery/childcarer, as it's usually right.
- Don't get too hung up about the external appearance of a nursery/childcarer – if the door needs a lick of paint, that has no bearing on the type of care your child will receive. Base your choice on a happy, relaxed, caring environment that has your child's interests at heart.

Anne-Marie has three children now aged eighteen, ten and four and comes from Hampshire.

> *I started using formal childcare in 1990 – a childminder for my then two-year-old and ten-year-old. I was a student at the time so cost was a bit of an issue. We found the childminder through word-of-mouth friend referral. I was lucky enough to have a supportive partner who could do a lot of the pick-ups and shared the load.*

Top tip:

- ➤ Be clear about what is important to you and prioritise the important things – no one is going to be 100 per cent as you would like – but you should make sure that your most important childcare needs are met. You may need to let go some things that are not as important to you.

Anne-Marie used to be a nanny herself and found that her experiences informed her relationship with her childcarer. She has some more tips for employers of nannies.

> *Be realistic – if it's OK for you to dump your children in front of the telly then it needs to be OK for your nanny to do so too. Remember that children need consistency, particularly in home-based childcare. You have to work with your nanny and agree boundaries – and don't ignore the boundaries at the weekend when you can't be bothered.*
>
> *I would also advise anyone to make sure their nanny is first-aid trained and either knows a lot about child development or has formal qualifications. I have met too many nannies who really shouldn't have been calling themselves nannies . . .*

Isabel and Andrew have children now aged four and one and live in Berkshire.

> *We started using a childminder when our first baby was five months old. I hadn't researched any of the options as I thought I'd have plenty of time when the baby was born (ha!) so it was difficult trawling around nurseries, childminders, etc., with a fussy, breastfeeding baby. I decided to use childminders because I wanted that homely feel. I wanted someone who I felt knew what they were doing, and in the end chose a 50-year-old childminder who had been doing it for 20 years and had her own grown-up son. Importantly to me, she was the kind of person who really liked to hold and cuddle the baby. When we moved to Berkshire, the children went to a lovely local nursery.*

Top tips:

- Research and decide as much as you can before you have a baby, not least because of waiting lists.
- The combination of childcare that you'll use over time will change from nurseries, nannies and childminders to after-school clubs, so don't get too hung up on the long term: things change quickly in a child's early life.
- Go with your values. I chose a nursery slightly shabbier than most (I hate that bleached white sterile environment where the staff wear rubber gloves to change nappies) because it seemed happy, warm and loving. OK, the piano was out of tune and the paint was peeling a bit but I can look past the cobwebs (and can admit to having some in my house!). If you don't like something, say so. Try to get a good look at mealtimes, too, to see the food, and how

closely staff help and encourage younger children to make sure they've eaten enough.

Louise is a single mother with children aged eight and five who lives in Kent.

When my son was two months old, I used a nanny. I returned to work part-time.

I found her through an ad in the Lady *magazine. In this instance, I relied on my own reference-checking skills – I think that if you have the time, and are thorough, you can do just as good a job as an agency. The only problem with the first nanny was that she had told me she didn't smoke but actually did – I felt she hadn't been truthful and that breakdown in trust meant I eventually replaced her.*

Subsequently some of the help I have hired have been housekeepers who assist with children, and the main issues have included not understanding English (but saying yes to everything!) and poor timekeeping. With children of school age, the housekeeping element becomes more important. Also, as I run my own business I can, in general, be flexible and available to do reading, homework, etc., with the children.

Top tips:

- Identify what your real childcare requirements are (for instance, if you have young children at home it may be unfair to expect your carer to do your laundry and other domestic chores as well).
- Invest in the best person for you and make them feel valued, irrespective of their training and experience.

- Take the time to show them how you like to do things in your home and with your children.
- Emphasise that honesty and communication are key.
- Remember that you will go through all the usual worries of any parent leaving a baby or young children with someone they do not know. Such concerns dissipate as you all get used to a new nanny or housekeeper.

Kathy and Paul have three children, now aged six, four and two, and live in Cheshire.

I started using childcare when my first baby, Anna, was six months old and I went back to work three days a week. I decided on a day nursery for two reasons: cost and safety. I was very uneasy about leaving a six-month-old, who would be unable to tell me about her day, with a nanny. I felt that at a day nursery there would be safety in numbers – if one carer was having a bad day, hopefully another would be having a good one; staying in one location reduced the risk of the baby being left on the bus (a story I had heard!); there were clear procedures that seemed to be followed well. I found the nursery through a friend's recommendation. I did visit a couple of others but this was the one in the most convenient location and I felt happy about the standard of care.

I continued to use the day nursery for three years (sending Lucy there, too, when she was six months) and was reasonably happy with the care. The girls were generally happy and enjoyed the social interaction. Some of the staff were very good, others less so, and there was quite a lot of change: I was concerned about continuity of carers. For me, the mornings and evenings were quite stressful, with a big rush to get out of the house in the morning and tired or hungry babies to pick up on my way home from work at 6 p.m., feed, bath, play with and get into bed around 7 p.m.

After I had Kate, I decided that the nursery would no longer be cost-effective or practical as Anna was due to start school a year later so I went down the nanny route. Finding one was hard. I didn't make it easy – I was looking for someone who wanted to work three days a week (Tuesday, Wednesday and Thursday) and look after three girls all under four. I signed up with a number of agencies but none was hopeful. Those who did find candidates told me I would have to pay quite a lot more per hour than the going rate due to my difficult brief.

In addition to the agencies, I put an ad on gumtree.com. I received a lot of responses. From a security perspective, I decided that I would request and contact referees before I invited anyone for interview. I saw around six candidates and found Dani, who has been with me ever since. Dani has been invaluable, to the extent that when she had a baby, we found a way to cover her maternity leave so that she could return to work with us: she brings the baby with her. She has a job that would have been hard to find with a baby, we have a nanny we love and trust, who is staying with us even though her job has changed – of the three girls, two are now at school and the youngest starts nursery soon.

Top tips:

- A nanny definitely makes the work–life balance easier. I can get up and go in the morning, regardless of the children's undressed state. And it's far easier in the evenings too, when I come back to find them fed and bathed.

- If you are prepared to put in the work checking references, CRB, getting registration for childcare vouchers, etc., then you can save a couple of thousand pounds on agency fees.

Emma and James are from Scotland and live in Norfolk with their three children, now aged nineteen, nine and five.

I made my choice based on information from the Childcare Information Service in Norwich, which was excellent and provided me with an up-to-date list of registered childminders, nurseries, playgroups, etc. Later, when I used nannies, I advertised on websites and in the local press. My concerns were availability and cost. I've rarely been concerned about quality of care: I'm often overwhelmed by the dedication and care of people working in the sector for relatively low wages.

For significant periods of time, costs have been crippling and I have hugely resented paying three sets of tax as the employer of a nanny. In your thirties and forties you can begin to make real progress in your career or your own business, and you often need to work atypical hours or travel to do so. Childcare to suit those ambitions is hard enough – but with triple tax it's so expensive that it's no wonder we have a glass ceiling! It's obvious, really – the triple tax on nannies is direct discrimination against women who have the audacity to be ambitious.

My first childminder parked kids in front of the telly, fed them biscuits and sweets and had to be replaced. The next was fabulous – she had a lovely creative sunny home where the kids could just be part of the family and eat mud in the garden!

My subsequent experiences were generally very positive, with the occasional hiccup. We used a great nursery for a while, and when the school run complicated things we found a fantastic nanny who never missed a day in three years – even walking two miles along snowbound roads to get to work on time.

Top tips:

- ➤ If your children cling to you when you're leaving, something's wrong and you need to change your arrangements. This has only happened to me twice in 19 years (the telly-childminder and a bad nursery experience when my child became distressed and came out in a rash). Somehow I never for a minute felt it was because I was leaving them in someone else's hands, I just presumed that the care wasn't good enough. I made other arrangements and everyone was happy again.
- ➤ If the mother is happy the children will be happier. Some mums would be miserable leaving their children; others, like me, would be miserable at home all day. It's definitely better for us that I'm a working mum.
- ➤ Trust and respect your childcarer. Never feel competitive: if your children love them that has to be great for your children – and that's the most important thing. Trust and respect, of course, means showing appreciation and care, but it also means respecting them as a professional, paying them properly and on time, respecting their time and personal space.
- ➤ Some people take the professional part a bit too far. I knew a management consultant who applied her performance-management techniques to her nannies.

None of them lasted more than a few months. I heard that the last told her to **** off and stormed out when she tried to sit her down for an appraisal! One-to-one childcare is too important and personal for appraisals – it has to be about mutual respect and real teamwork.

➤ My most successful childminders were initially not registered, just other mums I knew and admired as mothers and they eventually became registered childminders. I'm a great fan of childminders, if you can find the right person.

The Simpsons live in the Midlands with their two children, now aged six and four.

I went back to work when my first baby was six months old. I checked out a few nurseries and had a good feeling about the two I ended up using. The first was near my office, but as I work from different offices fairly routinely it became difficult to be tied to one location daily. I had thought originally it would be easier to use a nursery near the office but in the end it was easier to use one near home.

The one I selected near our home just felt right. I visited three and chose Noah's Ark because it had great facilities for the kids – farm animals on-site, a nature trail for them to walk along, which was away from roads, nice enclosed play area, great group of nursery nurses, and it was an independent nursery, not part of a chain. It was the most expensive of the three I looked at, though. My experience was very positive, even the illness issue – luckily my children were hardly ever ill so I didn't need to take any time off work to keep them at home.

Having two kids makes it more financially viable to have a nanny (it's too expensive when you have just one child). My nanny came from the nursery and already knew the kids. She was fantastic and I couldn't recommend her highly enough. Before my nanny arrived, I was concerned about the social interaction the children would get as they'd no longer be in a nursery with others. Now I can't believe I ever worried about this: nannies have networks and tend to socialise with others who have kids of a similar age. My kids had, and still do have, a better social life than I do!

I didn't want to make her redundant but couldn't justify paying a full-time nanny when the kids started full-time at school even though it does mean I now have a headache covering school holidays. We tried to arrange a nannyshare but couldn't find one that would work, and now make do with a sort of patchwork compromise.

Top tips:

- If you've never employed a nanny before, ask someone who has. It's only once you've done it that you realise what's involved and the sort of questions to ask at an interview.
- Budget at the outset. Childcare is very expensive. With a nursery, there is a set fee. With a nanny there are lots of outgoings. Not only is there the basic salary, but you have to pay additional tax and NI, cover their petrol and give them money for things like toddler groups, gym club, etc. You also have to do the tax calculations yourself or pay an agency to do them for you. It adds up to an awful lot!

Ellie and Tom have one baby, now 18 months, and live in Northamptonshire.

> *I went back to work when Bryn was five months old and chose a childminder. I looked on the government website, which listed all the local childminders. Initially I was concerned about carer-to-child ratio, which is always high with a childminder, but the lady we found was superb and adored Bryn so all went well.*
>
> *Although I felt very guilty about leaving my baby, I sometimes found at work I had moments of completely forgetting I had a child, which I found quite liberating. But I put that down to having such great peace of mind, and the right balance of work and motherhood (working three days a week). I found it amazing how little ones love the company of other little ones: I think Bryn developed much more quickly than if I had cared for him myself. The only bad points were rushing back to collect him – London transport really tested my nerves in the first few months back at work.*
>
> *When we moved up to Northampton, I found another good childminder. By this time Bryn was eleven months old and he found it a little more difficult to adjust, but after about three weeks of desperate screaming and me feeling like the worst mother in the world, he settled in and now really enjoys his time there. The bad points of childcare are when your baby isn't well and you have to either shift your working week, or not go in at all. That can sometimes be quite stressful but is all part of parenthood.*

Top tips:

- Whatever your instincts, go with them. I looked at several childminders and nurseries and opted for the one where I felt my child fitted in best. All children are different so no single option is right for all.
- A good tip a childminder gave me is to drop your child off, then go back a bit later (if you can) when they aren't expecting you – that way you get to see how the care really is without them being prepared for your return.

Conclusion
Where to Go from Here . . .

There is a lot more to finding childcare than first meets the eye. Choosing the type of care that suits you and your child, as well as your wallet, can be a challenge, and is one reason that many parents make changes in their working life: they have to fit in with their childcare arrangements. Only a thorough understanding of the options available will reassure you that you are making the right choice, and I hope that this book has gone some way to providing that. I realise that in most cases two parents will be involved in making the final decision, not to mention a number of children with different personalities, needs and preferences. The most important thing to remember is to give the decision-making process the time, consideration and space it deserves, and to find a solution that makes practical and financial sense and feels instinctively right. Then, with the arrangements in place, you will be able to walk confidently back into the workplace with a new string to your bow: parenthood.

Appendix 1: Contracts of Employment

SAMPLE CONTRACT OF EMPLOYMENT BETWEEN NANNY AND EMPLOYER

Parties:

.... and ....
(together hereinafter referred to as 'the Employer')

.... (hereinafter referred to as 'the Employee')

Job title
The Employee is employed by the Employer as [nanny/after-school carer/mother's help] to look after [ ] (hereinafter referred to as 'the Children').

Date of commencement of employment ....
No period of employment with a previous employer counts

towards the Employee's period of continuous employment. [The employment of the Employee is for a fixed period intended to end on [ ] and in the absence of any agreement to the contrary the employment will terminate on that date without the requirement for notice to be given to that effect by either party.]

Place of work .... [The Employee shall not be required to travel on holiday with the Employer, unless agreed.] [The Employee may be required to accompany the family on holiday in the United Kingdom [and overseas].]

Hours of work
It is intended that the Employee will work [on .... /each weekday] between the hours of .... and .... each day, but it is accepted by both parties that circumstances such as emergencies may mean that these hours vary from time to time. [In the school holidays and occasionally at other times it may be necessary to adjust the Employee's hours of work. Any arrangements to work such extra hours, including babysitting, will be agreed in advance with as much notice as possible.]

Job description
The Employee shall perform such duties as the Employer may reasonably request from time to time to include the following general duties:

1. looking after the Children's needs, welfare, development and health and safety
2. supervision of the Children
3. exercise, teaching and training

4. playing with the Children
5. encouraging developmental skills, such as reading, writing, arithmetic, drawing, music, dressing and telling the time
6. taking the Children to and from nursery/school
7. nursery duties, including keeping the Children's rooms and communal areas tidy, the Children's laundry, shopping and cooking for the Children's meals
8. keeping a diary of the Children's activities [and meals]

and the Employee shall observe the following House Rules:

- The house is a no-smoking house.
- [When the house is left empty, the alarm must be set.]
- Any breakages must be reported immediately or as soon as possible.
- [For live-ins, include rules about when washing-machine can be used, overnight guests, playing music, keeping room clean, etc.]

The Employee shall never delegate her duties to anyone else without the Employer's prior knowledge and agreement. The Employer reserves the right to vary the Employee's duties at any time, provided that any such variation is reasonable.

Car and telephone

Either [A car will be made available to the Employee for the purposes of her employment [and for personal use].] The Employer shall be responsible for putting the required insurance in place and will pay all expenses connected thereto including petrol costs [while the Employee is discharging her duties], except parking fines, speeding fines or fines for clamps/towing away. [If the Employee is involved in an accident in which it is not possible to claim against a third party, she will be required to pay the excess due for any claim and the Employer shall be entitled to deduct such sum from her salary.]

Or [The Employee shall provide her own fully and comprehensively insured car in order to fulfil her duties and shall log in the log book provided by the Employer the mileage for each journey, such mileage to be compensated at the rate of [40p] per mile. The Employee shall ensure that her car is properly serviced and that any mechanical fault is promptly repaired. The Employer will provide car seats for use by the Children when they are in the Employee's car, and these should be fitted and maintained in accordance with the manufacturer's instructions.]

The Employee warrants that she holds a full clean valid driving licence and that she will immediately notify the Employer in the event that she is prosecuted for any road traffic offence, if the licence is endorsed, or if she is disqualified from driving.

The Employee shall only use the telephone for calls related to her employment – personal calls are to be made only in an emergency or with the Employer's prior consent.

[The use of email and the Internet on the Employer's computer is strictly limited to the purpose of the Children's learning and education with the Employer's prior agreement.]

Salary

The Employee shall be paid in arrears the sum of .... [before the deduction of tax and National Insurance contributions

(NICs), in cash/by cheque/by standing order] [every day/on or around the [last/first] working day of each week/ month]. The Employer will be responsible for accounting for the Employer's and Employee's income tax and NICs. [A salary review will take place on or around .... in each year.] [The Employee will be entitled to overtime pay at a rate of £....... per hour, such rate to apply also to any extra hours worked during school holidays and babysitting. Overtime will not be payable unless it is expressly agreed in advance. As noted above, it is accepted by the parties that there will need to be some degree of flexibility in the daily working hours and the Employee will not receive overtime payments for any additional hours worked as a result unless expressly agreed in advance.] The Employee will be reimbursed all reasonable expenses properly incurred in the course of employment and authorised by the Employer on the production of receipts or such other evidence as the Employer shall reasonably require. The Employee shall generally be provided with a kitty for any such expenditure incurred.

[[Accommodation and] meals [live-in only]]
[The Employee's accommodation consists of .... which she will occupy under a licence. Upon the termination of her employment, she will be required to vacate the accommodation on the last day of her employment.]

[The Employee will be provided with food and beverages when on duty.]

Holiday
[Note that the minimum holiday entitlement is four weeks per annum plus bank holidays.]

The Employee will be entitled to .... [weeks'/days'] paid holiday each calendar year, to be arranged with the agreement of the Employer [and to be taken within school holidays]. This [will/will not] include any bank holidays falling on days upon which the Employee would otherwise work. No holiday entitlement may be carried over to the following year and no more than [10] days' holiday may be taken at any one time without the Employer's prior agreement. The Employer shall nominate [10] days in a year on which the Employee's entitlement must be used. Both the Employer and the Employee must give as much notice as possible (but at least one month) of holidays being taken.

Sickness
The Employer will pay the Employee statutory sick pay in accordance with legislation in force. Any additional sick pay will be made at the discretion of the Employer. The Employee agrees to notify the Employer as soon as possible if she is unavoidably prevented from coming to work and in any event at least one hour prior to the time she is due to commence work on each day she is unable to work.

Compassionate leave
The Employer will consider all reasonable requests for compassionate leave and time off to deal with family emergencies. Any payment for time taken off in such circumstances will be made at the Employer's discretion.

Insurance
The Employer is insured against claims for personal injury. The Employee is advised to arrange her own insurance for claims

against professional negligence. [The Professional Association of Nursery Nurses can arrange insurance for qualified nannies, but other carers are advised to contact their usual insurer in the first instance.]

Notice period
For the first month of employment, the contract is terminable by one week's written notice on either side. Thereafter the notice period shall be one month for the first four years of employment, increasing to five weeks after five years of continuous employment and by an additional week per complete year worked thereafter to a maximum of twelve weeks after twelve years' continuous employment. These notice periods shall not apply in the event of gross misconduct.

Confidentiality
The Employee will at all times keep the affairs and business of the Employer confidential.

Pensions
The Employer does not run a pension scheme and the employment is not contracted out of the state earnings related pension scheme.

Grievance
Any grievance that the Employee may have should normally be discussed with the Employer in the first instance. If the Employee wishes to raise the grievance formally, she should set out the basis of the grievance in writing. A hearing at which she may be accompanied by an appropriate person will be held to

discuss the grievance. The Employer will set out in writing the outcome of the hearing and the Employee will have the right to appeal that decision.

Dismissal
The Employer reserves the right to dismiss the Employee without notice in the event of gross misconduct which shall without limitation include the following circumstances:

- use of drugs or alcohol during hours of employment or attending work under the influence of drugs or alcohol
- physical, psychological or emotional abuse of the Children
- violent or threatening behaviour
- gross neglect of the Children
- theft, fraud or other dishonesty
- gross incompetence
- insubordination
- material breach of the terms of this agreement
- behaviour which is incompatible with or prejudicial to the job, or which is likely to cause injury to the Employer or the Children or the Employer's property
- logging on to sexually explicit websites or downloading pornography from the Internet using the Employer's facilities and/or during working hours

Before taking any disciplinary action the Employer will ordinarily (unless the circumstances preclude such process in the Employer's reasonable opinion) provide full details of the complaint in writing and to give the Employee a reasonable opportunity to state her case at a hearing at which she may be accompanied by an appropriate person. The Employer reserves the right to suspend the Employee during any disciplinary process. The decision of the hearing will be confirmed in writing and the Employee will have the right to appeal that decision.

Entire Agreement

This agreement sets out the entire agreement relating to the Employee's employment and the Employee entering into this agreement is not relying on any representations or warranties not set out herein. There are no collective agreements relating to the Employee's employment and any variations to this agreement must be in writing.

Signature of Parties

.... On behalf of the Employer

Dated...................

.... (Employee)

Dated...................

Appendix 2: Finances

For the latest up-to-date figures on tax credits and voucher schemes go to www.direct.gov.uk and follow the links. The Daycare Trust website (www.daycaretrust.org.uk) is also an excellent source of this information.

EMPLOYER-SUPPORTED CHILDCARE

There are three ways in which employers can support staff with their childcare costs, which can save both you and your employer money through tax and National Insurance contribution (NIC) exemptions. These are:

- childcare vouchers: up to £55 per week (£243 per month)
- payments to childcare providers: up to £55 per week (£243 per month)
- workplace childcare provision: up to the full amount for which the employer subsidises the childcare

The following conditions apply.

- An employer must provide the support to a parent.
- The employee must have an 'eligible' child. A child qualifies up to 1 September following their 15th birthday; or if the child is disabled, up to 1 September following their 16th birthday. The number of children in the family makes no difference to the amount of the exemption.
- The childcare used must be 'registered or approved'.

ELIGIBILITY

The exemptions are only available on the support outlined above, and not for any other types of support. None of the following is eligible: cash payments to employees to cover childcare costs; payments towards school fees; payments to a close relative who is not a registered or approved childcarer.

HOW EMPLOYERS CAN PROVIDE THE EXEMPTION

(a) *In addition to salary* This pays an amount on top of an employee's existing salary. It is the most beneficial to employees, as they benefit from the employer's subsidy as well as the tax and NIC exemptions. This costs the employer more.

(b) *Salary sacrifice* An employee gives up salary in exchange for the employer contributing an equivalent amount to a childcare place or a childcare voucher.

VOUCHER SCHEMES

Your employer will normally sign up to a childcare voucher scheme and will pay the scheme operator an administration fee for their service. The operator will either supply you directly with your childcare vouchers or will provide your employer with them, and they will distribute to staff accordingly in paper or electronic form (or, in some cases, pay the provider direct). Employees may then use them to 'pay' their nanny or other registered form of childcare. The nanny will then redeem the value of the voucher from the childcare voucher company, usually by direct payment into her bank account.

Each parent can claim, thereby doubling the amount of benefit to £110 a week and maximum annual tax relief to £2,390 for two higher-rate earners (each basic-rate taxpayer can save £962 a year). Use persuasion if your employer doesn't offer these childcare vouchers – remind them this means they won't have to pay NICs on the portion of your salary you take in vouchers.

Employers aren't obliged to offer the vouchers but, in many cases, a straightforward request will work as the administration is not too onerous either. You can't claim vouchers if you are paying a relative, nanny or other person who's *not* registered with Ofsted.

If your employer provides you with childcare vouchers you will not have to pay tax or NICs on the first £55 per week, or £243 per month. However, if your vouchers are worth more than this, you will have to pay tax and NICs on the remainder.

You do not have to use childcare vouchers in the week or month they are provided. You can save them up to use later – for example during school holidays when childcare costs are higher.

You need to have received your childcare voucher or vouchers before you can use them. They cannot be backdated. For example, if your nursery fees are due on 1 May and you get your first voucher on 15 May, you can only use the childcare voucher for your next fees due on 1 June.

When you first join a voucher scheme, it may take some time to set up. You may find that the cash element of your salary has been reduced before you receive your vouchers. If you think you should have started to receive vouchers, or you don't receive them when you expect to, contact the voucher provider as soon as possible. You will find a helpline number on the information pack sent to you by the provider when you first joined the scheme.

If you use electronic childcare vouchers, the scheme operator may ask you to authorise payment to the childcare provider on a monthly or other basis. You need to authorise this payment to make sure your childcare provider is paid. If you forget, you may be asked to make up the shortfall in some other way.

DIRECTLY CONTRACTED CHILDCARE

In directly contracted childcare your employer arranges with a childcare provider to provide childcare to you. Where this happens, the same limits of £55 per week, or £243 per month, apply. This means your employer can pay a childcare provider up to these amounts and you will not have to pay tax or NICs on that sum. However, if your employer pays more for your directly contracted childcare, you will have to pay tax and NICs on the remainder.

These limits apply to each individual employee, which

means that you are only entitled to one exempt amount regardless of the number of jobs or employments you may have. If both you and your partner receive childcare vouchers, you are each entitled to an exempt amount. For more information about these salary sacrifice schemes visit www.hmrc.gov.uk

FINANCING PRESCHOOL COSTS

All three- and four-year-olds are entitled to 12.5 hours of free early-years education per week for 38 weeks per year with a 'registered provider', such as a school, nursery or playgroup, regardless of income or circumstances. This entitlement is currently expanding to two-year-olds in some disadvantaged areas. Some large employers provide registered early-years education at the workplace.

TAX CREDITS FOR WORKING PARENTS

Working Tax Credit is a top-up on wages for people on low incomes – whether they are employed or self-employed – and can include support for childcare. Many working families may receive help with their childcare costs through the childcare element of Working Tax Credit. If you use registered or approved childcare and work more than 16 hours per week, depending on your income, you could claim back up to 80 per cent of your childcare costs.

There are limits on the weekly costs you can claim. If you pay childcare for:

- one child, the maximum you can claim is £175 a week
- two or more children, the maximum is £300 a week

Families may also be able to get help through Child Tax Credit – a means-tested allowance for parents and carers with incomes of less than £66,000.

More information is available on the Tax Credit Helpline (0845 300 3900) or on the website: www.taxcredits.inlandrevenue.gov.uk

Not sure if you'll be better off with childcare vouchers or tax credits? (You can't have both!) Normally, if you get tax credits of more than £545 a year (£1,090 in your child's first year) it is better to opt for tax credits than vouchers. Use the calculator at www.hmrc.gov.uk/calcs/ccin.htm to check what's best for you.

Child tax credit and the child-related elements of working tax credit are paid to the main carer. If you are self-employed, tax credits are paid directly by HM Revenue & Customs. The self-employed can't receive childcare vouchers but directors of companies can have them, so long as they are available to other employees of the company, too.

HELP FOR STUDENTS

If you're in further education, you may be able to get extra financial help through the Care to Learn Scheme (for students under 20) or through Learner Support Funds. There's also a scheme providing help with childcare costs for sixth-form students aged 20 or over. As a higher-education student, you may be eligible for extra help on top of any standard student loans or grants you receive. This may include a bursary, Child Tax Credit,

Childcare Grant, or help from the Access to Learning Fund.

Money may also be available through educational trusts or charities. Ask your student welfare adviser or local authority for guidance.

Appendix 3: Children with Special Needs

Childcare services are required by law to cater for children with disabilities. When registering, they should state what facilities they have to cater for children with special needs. Unfortunately the Daycare Trust reports that, while most providers say they can cater for special needs at the time of registration, many parents say that the providers can't offer a special-needs place when it's required.

Legally, childcare providers are not allowed to treat a disabled child less favourably than other children because of their disability. For example, this means that they cannot stop a disabled child coming on an outing or charge more for a disabled child without a good financial reason. They must also make 'reasonable adjustments' to their services and facilities so that disabled children can use them. This may include adapting premises to make them wheelchair accessible, training staff to use special equipment, or setting up special meal arrangements for a child with a severe food allergy.

Your first port of call when looking for care for a child with special needs should be your local Children's Information Service (through Childcare Link: www.childcarelink.gov.uk) who can provide listings of the childcare services available. Some areas may have childcare services especially tailored for children with disabilities and special educational needs while in others services are inclusive within existing childcare provision.

You should also speak to the local Early Years Development and Childcare Partnership (EYDCP). Many providers who have a childcare place available can't offer it because they lack the facilities, staff or assistance that may be required to provide a quality place for a child. Some EYDCPs have funding specifically to assist childcare places for children with disabilities or special needs. It can often be used to pay for additional staff or specific equipment.

Talk to potential providers about any special needs your child has, such as dietary requirements or medical assistance. Discuss with them how best they can meet your child's needs. Think about whether your carer will need special training to care for your child. See if you can arrange a settling-in period or spend some time with the carer so that you, the carer and your child can get to know each other. Think also about how you will get your child to and from their carer. Some childminders or out-of-school clubs may be willing to pick up your child from school, but you may have to be responsible for getting your child there.

Parent partnership services These provide support and advice to parents whose children have special educational needs, particularly during the assessment process. They provide accurate and unbiased information on the full range of options and are there to help you make informed decisions about your child's care and education.

Home visiting services There are a number of different types of home visiting service.

- Some local authorities have teams of teachers working as part of an Early Years Inclusion Team.
- Sure Start children's centres also have support workers who visit families at home.
- Families can also receive regular visits through Home Start, which offers a network of trained parent volunteers who support parents needing extra help for many different reasons, including illness or disability of their children or the parents themselves.

Portage is another home visiting educational service for preschool children with additional support needs and their families. It takes place in the child's home, equipping parents with the skills and confidence to help their child. Portage home visitors may be teachers, speech or occupational therapists, nursery nurses, health visitors, community nurses, social workers, parents or volunteers with relevant experience. They are all trained by the National Portage Association. These schemes run in many areas. You can find out more by contacting the National Portage Association on 01935 471 641 (Monday and Thursday, 9 a.m. to 1 p.m.).

Appendix 4: List of EEA Countries

Austria
Belgium
Cyprus
Czech Republic
Denmark
Estonia
Finland
France
Germany
Greece
Hungary
Ireland
Italy
Latvia
Lithuania
Luxembourg
Malta
Poland
Netherlands
Portugal
Slovak Republic
Slovenia
Spain
Sweden
United Kingdom
Iceland*
Liechtenstein*
Norway*
Switzerland**

* These countries are in the EEA, but are not members of the European Union.
** Switzerland is not in the EEA but an international treaty means that Swiss nationals have a similar right to live in the UK as EEA nationals.

Appendix 5: Childcare Qualifications

The main recognised childcare qualifications are:

- CACHE Level 3, Diploma in Childcare and Education (DCE) (previously known as NNEB), a two-year full-time or three-year part-time course equivalent to two A levels
- BTEC Higher National Diploma: a full-time course equivalent of the first year of a degree
- NVQ in Childcare and Education, Level 3: considered the equivalent of the CACHE Level 3 Diploma. An experienced childminder or mother's help could apply to be assessed at this level
- City & Guilds vocational courses
- Montessori diploma

CACHE is the Council for Awards in Children's Care and Education. They are a specialist body that develops courses and qualifications in childcare. They have three roles:

- to write and assess training courses for new entrants to the childcare, education and playwork professions
- to accredit the competence of childcarers and play-workers in their workplace
- to raise the standard of children's care and education and playwork

Awards include:
CACHE Foundation Award in Caring for Children (CFCC)
A taster course giving an introduction to the type of knowledge and understanding required when working in childcare.

CACHE Level 2, Certificate in Childcare and Education (CCE)
A one-year full-time or two-year part-time course for students wanting to be childcare assistants. Having gained the certificate, they may progress to other qualifications such as CACHE Diploma in Childcare and Education or, once working, to the Level 3 NVQ in Early Years Care and Education, which offers assessment in the workplace.

CACHE Level 3, Diploma in Childcare and Education (DCE) (previously known as NNEB)
This is a two-year full-time or three-year part-time course and is equivalent to two A levels. The course takes two years to complete and covers health, safety, nutrition and educational play for ages up to seven. Around 60 per cent of students' time is spent in college and the remaining 40 per cent with different-age children on placements in homes, day nurseries, hospitals and junior schools. Around half of those who graduate with the diploma will go on to work in local authority or private day

nurseries and hospitals while the rest will become nannies with families. It can also be used as an entry-level qualification to midwifery training, provided the candidate has GCSE grade C in English language, and mathematics or a science subject. Moving into teaching or social work is another option with the diploma.

CACHE Level 3 Certificate in Childminding Practice (CCP)
This course develops the knowledge and skills of anyone who is, or is looking to become, a registered childminder; introduced by the National Childminding Association (NCMA).

BTEC (Business and Technology Education Council):
vocational qualifications organised and awarded by the
Edexcel Foundation. Courses include:
BTEC National Diploma Childhood Studies (Nursery Nursing)
BTEC Higher National Diploma (HND) Childhood Studies (Nursery Nursing)
BTEC National Certificate Childhood Studies (Nursery Nursing)
BTEC Higher National Certificate Childhood Studies (Nursery Nursing)
The BTEC First Certificate

NVQ in Early Years Care and Education
This is a government initiative to give people with experience but no formal qualification the opportunity to get a recognised qualification. It is not an academic qualification but based on practical experience in the workplace where students have to prove that they have achieved a certain level of competence and capability. Students have to complete fifteen modules and

courses can take up to two years to complete. Candidates can take as long as they need to complete the award.

NVQ in Childcare and Education Level 2

This qualification is awarded to a childcare worker in a supervised role – for example, a nursery assistant. Students register with an NVQ accredited centre and start to gain the 'modules' required by being assessed in the workplace. Eventually they build up a portfolio of 'evidence' to demonstrate ability and competence to the assessors. Students are assessed on one of four 'endorsements':

- Work with Babies
- Work in Support of Others
- Work in a Preschool Group
- Work in a Community Run Preschool Group

A nanny would be likely to choose Work with Babies or Work in a Preschool Group and would acquire an NVQ in Childcare and Education (Work with Babies Level 2).

NVQ in Childcare and Education Level 3

This could be considered the equivalent of an NNEB. A childcarer undertaking this training shows a commitment to learning about high-quality childcare. There are five 'endorsements':

- Group Care and Education
- Preschool Provision
- Family Support
- Special Needs
- Family Day Care

A nanny would choose Family Day Care to give her an NVQ in Childcare and Education (Family Day Care) Level 3.

NVQ Level 4
This is undertaken by a childcare worker who would already be trained to management level. More academically challenging, it consists of three strands: Advanced Practice; Enhancing Quality; and Quality Control and Management.

Maternity Nurse Courses (NVQ Level 3)
This three-month intensive course includes emergency first-aid, prevention of sudden infant death syndrome, post-natal care of mother and child, breastfeeding support, baby massage and maternal and infant nutrition.

Norland, Chiltern and Princess Christian
These are private, residential colleges with their own nurseries for training on site. The two-year course includes a period of between six and nine months during which a nanny is placed within a family.

Introduction to Childcare Practice
This short course usually takes place over a couple of days and will give a nanny the basic training and the certificate she needs to register with Ofsted (see page 321).

City & Guilds
City & Guilds administers GNVQ courses: vocational courses equivalent to A levels.

NAMCW (National Association of Maternal and Child Welfare)
This was a two-year course (now obsolete but can be found on CVs), which involved practical experience and attendance at college. It was very similar to the DCE but covered all ages up to teens. Topics included special needs, and the student qualified for a supervisory role within nurseries. The NAMCW is not generally recognised as a substantial enough qualification to work in a day nursery.

Montessori
The Montessori Method is an internationally renowned qualification. It is a method and philosophy that gives much individual attention to the child and his/her needs and encourages them to develop at their own pace. It is a holistic curriculum that aims to develop the child socially, intellectually, physically and emotionally.

To graduate as a Montessori teacher, students need a minimum of a college degree and a year's student teaching under supervision.

NB: Courses are changing all the time. The government is currently restructuring the framework of qualifications for those who want to work in childcare. For up-to-date information, contact the Qualifications and Curriculum Authority (QCA), the body responsible for implementing these changes, at: www.qca.org.uk

Resources

Please note: The following section has been compiled by way of general guidance only. It is not an exhaustive list nor is it a substitute for or to be relied on for specific expert advice. Readers are advised to use Internet search engines and rely on recommendations when looking for childcare services or information on childcare provision. So far as the author is aware the information given is correct and up to date as at May 2009.

AU PAIRS

AGENCIES

The following au pair agencies are members of BAPAA. Most agencies operate nationally, wherever they are based geographically. See the website for more information on au pairs.

International Recruitment Agency Ltd
200 High Road, Wood Green, London N22 8HH
Contact: Marcia Behseta
Tel: +44 (0)208 889 2010
Email: aaupair@aol.com
Web: www.aaupair.com

Help Unlimited
The Old Rectory, Suffield, Norfolk NR11 7EW
Contact: Anna de Soissons
Tel: +44 (0)1263 768 675 / (0)1263 834 290
Email: info@helpunlimited.co.uk
Web: www.helpunlimited.co.uk

Janet White Agency
67 Jackson Avenue, Leeds, West Yorkshire LS8 1NS
Contact: Janet White
Tel: +44 (0)113 266 6507
Fax: +44 (0)113 268 3077
Email: info@janetwhite.com
Web: www.janetwhite.com

Just Au Pairs (Inc. Au Pairs by Avalon & A-One Au-Pairs & Nannies)
35 The Grove, Edgware, Middlesex HA8 9QA
Contact: Hilary Perry
Freephone: 0800 298 8807
Tel: +44 (0)208 905 4400 / +44 (0)208 905 3355
Fax: +44 (0)208 905 3838
Email: info@justaupairs.co.uk or info@aupairsetc.co.uk
Web: www.justaupairs.co.uk
www.aupairsbyavalon.co.uk
www.aupairsetc.co.uk

Language Studies Network Ltd (trading as ICEPWORLD LONDON)
Suite 3, 37 Great Russell Street, London WC1B 3PP
Contact: Mr Celemet Yener
Tel: +44 (0)207 580 3106
Fax: +44 (0)870 288 9535
Email: uk@icepworld.com
Web: www.icepworld.com

Millennium Au Pairs & Nannies
The Coach House, The Crescent, Belmont, Sutton,
Surrey SM2 6BP
Contact: Jackie Gallacher
Tel: +44 (0)208 241 9752
Fax: +44 (0)208 643 1268
Email: info:info@millenniumaupairs.co.uk
Web: www.millenniumaupairs.co.uk

Peek-a-Boo Au Pairs & Nannies
5th Floor, 13–14 King Street, Bank, London EC2V 8EA
Contact: Ms Sara Rahmani
Tel: +44 (0)207 600 9880
Email: sara@peekaboochildcare.com
Web: www.peekaboochildcare.com

Peter Pan Au Pairs
The Greys, Erriottwood, Lynsted, Kent ME9 OJW
Contact: Nicola Price
Tel: +44 (0)1795 886475
Fax: +44 (0)1795 886146
Email: nicky@peterpan-aupairs.com
Web: www.peterpanaupairs.co.uk

Quick Aupair & Nanny Agency
22 The Ridings, Norwich NR4 6UJ
Contact: Bryan Levy
Tel: +44 (0)1603 50 34 34
Fax: +44 (0)7092 03 98 731
Email: office@quickaupair.co.uk
Web: www.quickaupair.co.uk

Quickhelp Agency Ltd
307a Finchley Road, London NW3 6EH
Contact: Norma Cutner
Tel: +44 (0)207 794 8666
Fax: +44 (0)207 433 1993
Email: mailbox@quickhelp.freeserve.co.uk
Web: www.quickhelp.co.uk

Richmond and Twickenham Au Pairs and Nannies
The Old Rectory, Savey Lane, Yoxall, Burton-on-Trent, Staffs DE13 8PD
Contact: Vicki Whitwell
Tel: +44 (0)1543 473828
Fax: +44 (0)1543 473838
Email: karen@aupairsnationwide.co.uk
Web: www.aupairsnationwide.co.uk

Smart Au Pairs
Wealden Barn, Pett Lane, Charing, Kent TN27 0DS
Contact: Nicole Kofkin
Tel : +44 (0)1233 712 500
Email: nicole@smartaupairs.com
Web: www.smartaupairs.com

Sunny Smiles Au Pair Agency
P O Box 280, Sevenoaks, Kent TN13 1FU
Contact: Kamila Lasakova-Walker
Tel: +44 (0)1732 452 282
Fax: +44 (0)1732 452 282
Email: info@sunnysmiles.co.uk
Web: www.sunnysmiles.co.uk

The Au-Pair Agency
231 Hale Lane, Edgware, Middlesex HA8 9QF
Contact: Elaine Newman
Tel: +44 (0)208 958 1750
Fax: +44 (0)208 958 5261
Email: elaine@aupairagency.com
Web: www.aupairagency.com

The Childcare Company (trading as Au Pair Selection)
7 Garth Road, Sevenoaks, Kent TN13 1RT
Contact: Mary Elder
Tel: 0844 800 6529
Email: enquiries@aupairselection.com
Web: www.aupairselection.com

The London Au Pair & Nanny Agency
4 Sunnyside, Childs Hill, Hampstead, London NW2 2QN
Contact: Mrs Maggie Dyer
Tel: +44 (0)207 435 3891
Email: londonaupair.nannyagency@virgin.net
Web: www.londonnanny.co.uk

The Specialist Au Pair Company Limited
171 Loxley Road, Stratford upon Avon, Warwickshire
CV37 7DT
Contact: Niranjani Osborne
Tel: 0845 602 5869
Email: niranjani@specialistaupaircompany.com
Web: www.specialistaupaircompany.com

A2Z Au Pairs
Catwell House, Catwell, Williton, Somerset TA4 4PF
Contact: Rebecca Haworth-Wood
Tel: +44 (0)8456 445506
Fax: +44 (0)1984 639013
Email: enquiries@a2zaupairs.com
Web: www.a2zaupairs.com

ABC Au Pairs
1 Childs Lane, London SE19 3RZ
Contact: Marina Lister
Tel: +44 (0)208 771 1918
Email: marina@abc-aupairs.co.uk
Web: www.abc-aupairs.co.uk

Angel Au Pairs
Unit 5 Dares Farm, Farnham Road, Ewshot, Farnham, Surrey GU10 5BB
Contact: Sue Warwick
Tel: +44 (0)1252 851978/851279
Fax: +44 (0)1252 851308
Email: mail@angelaupairs.com
Web: www.angelaupairs.com

Au Pair in America
37 Queen's Gate, London SW7 5HR
Contact: Marcie Schneider
Tel: +44 (0)207 581 73050
Fax: +44 (0)207 581 7355
Email: info@aupairamerica.co.uk
Web: www.aupairamerica.co.uk

Au Pair Network International
1 Northumberland Avenue, London WC2N 6BW
Contact: Mario Ristovski
Tel: +44 (0)203 239 7778
Fax: +44 (0)207 871 9533
Email: mario@apni.co.uk
Web: www.apni.co.uk

Au Pairs Direct
7 Little Meadow Road, Bowdon, Cheshire WA14 3PG
Contact: Andrea Conrad
Tel: +44 (0)161 941 5356
Fax: +44 (0)161 929 0102
Email: enquiries@aupairsdirect.co.uk
Web: www.aupairsdirect.co.uk

Bunters Ltd Au Pair and Nannies
The Old Malt House, 6 Church Street, Pattishall, Nr Towcester, Northampton NN2 8NB
Contact: Caroline Jones
Tel: +44 (0)1327 831 144
Fax: +44 (0)1327 831 155
Email: office@aupairsnannies.com
Web: www.aupairsnannies.com

Busybee Au Pairs Ltd
Carpenters Cottage, The Common, East Hanningfield, Chelmsford, Essex CM3 8AQ
Contact: Jamie Pullum
Tel: +44 (0)1245 401238
Fax: +44 (0)1245 403013
Email: jamie@busybeeaupairs.com
Web: www.busybeeaupairs.co.uk

Childcare International Ltd
Trafalgar House, Grenville Place, London NW7 3SA
Contact: Sandra Landau
Tel: +44 (0)208 906 3116
Fax: +44 (0)208 906 3461
Email: office@childint.co.uk
Web: www.childint.co.uk

VISA INFORMATION

www.ukvisas.gov.uk/en/

GENERAL CHILDCARE ADVICE

ChildcareLink
www.childcarelink.gov.uk

Directgov
www.direct.gov.uk

Sure Start
www.surestart.gov.uk

Daycare Trust
National childcare campaign.
www.daycaretrust.org.uk

BBC
Childcare section of BBC website.
www.bbc.co.uk/parenting

Every Child Matters
www.everychildmatters.gov.uk

Department for Children, Schools and Families
www.dcsf.gov.uk

Scottish Childcare
www.scottishchildcare.gov.uk

REGISTRATION AND INSPECTION OF CHILDCARE SETTINGS

In England
Ofsted
www.ofsted.gov.uk

In Wales
The Care and Social Services Inspectorate
www.csiw.wales.gov.uk

Childcare Approval Scheme
www.childcareapprovalschemewales.co.uk

In Scotland

The Scottish Commission for the Regulation of Care
www.carecommission.com

Her Majesty's Inspectorate of Education
www.hmie.gov.uk

In Northern Ireland

The Education and Training Inspectorate
www.etini.gov.uk

CHILDMINDERS

National Childminding Association (England and Wales)
www.ncma.org.uk

Scottish Childminding Association
www.childminding.org

Northern Ireland Childminding Association
www.nicma.org

DOULAS

Doula UK
www.doula.org.uk

British Doulas
www.britishdoulas.co.uk

Scottish Doula Network
www.scottishdoulanetwork.co.uk
Area covered: throughout Scotland, Northern England and Ireland

EMERGENCY CHILDCARE

www.emergencychildcare.co.uk
This site matches parents looking for childcare with NCMA members close to them. Parents can be confident that all childminders registered on the site are members of NCMA, and work to NCMA's Quality Standards.

NANNIES, MATERNITY NURSES AND MOTHERS' HELPS

A list of nanny agencies is not practical to include here, but Google is a good starting point for agencies in your area.

RECRUITMENT WEBSITES

www.bestbear.co.uk
www.nannyjob.co.uk
www.gumtree.com
www.greatcare.co.uk

NANNY PAYROLL COMPANIES

www.nannytax.co.uk
www.nannypayroll.co.uk
www.payefornannies.co.uk
www.nannypaye.co.uk

INSURANCE FOR NANNIES

www.mortonmichel.com
www.nannyinsure.co.uk

MALE NANNIES

www.mybigbuddy.com
Agency specialising in male nannies.

www.sharkyandgeorge.co.uk
Parties and holiday care for children between seven and fourteen.

NANNYSHARES

www.thenannysharers.co.uk
www.greatcare.co.uk

NURSERIES, WORKPLACE CHILDCARE, CHILDREN'S CENTRES AND PLAYGROUPS

National Day Nurseries Association
www.ndna.org.uk

Bright Horizons
www.brighthorizons.com

Employers for Childcare
www.employersforchildcare.org

Childcare Vouchers
www.childcarevouchers.co.uk

Pre-school Learning Alliance
www.pre-school.org.uk

4Children
www.4children.org.uk

SOSCN (Scotland)
Scottish charity supporting school-age play, care and learning.
www.soscn.org

Scottish Preschool Play Association
www.sppa.org.uk

Northern Ireland Preschool Playgroups Association
www.nippa.org

Clybiau Plant Cymru Kids' Clubs (Wales)
www.clybiauplantcymru.org

Wales Preschool Playgroups Association
www.walesppa.org

MATERNITY RIGHTS

www.worksmart.org.uk/rights/maternity_leave
www.direct.gov.uk/en/Employment/Employees/WorkAndFamilies/DG_10029285
www.businesslink.gov.uk/bdotg/action/layer?r.s=sl&topicId=1074045869

PARENTAL LEAVE

www.direct.gov.uk/en/Parents/Moneyandworkentitlements/Parentalleaveandpay/DG_10029416

FLEXIBLE WORKING

www.direct.gov.uk/en/Employment/Employees/

EMPLOYMENT RIGHTS

Directgov
www.direct.gov.uk

The Advisory, Conciliation and Arbitration Service (ACAS)
www.acas.org

TAX CREDITS

www.taxcredits.inlandrevenue.gov.uk

CHILDCARE COURSES

Council for Awards in Children's Care and Education (CACHE)
www.cache.org.uk

BTEC
www.edexcel.org.uk

Chiltern College
www.chilterncollege.com

Norland College
www.norland.co.uk

The National Childminding Association
www.ncma.org.uk

Scottish Childcare
www.scottishchildcare.co.uk

Royal Society for the Promotion of Health
www.rsph.org

Montessori Centre International
www.montessori.org.uk

City & Guilds
www.city-and-guilds.co.uk

FIRST-AID COURSES

www.redcrossfirstaidtraining.co.uk
www.aid-training.co.uk
www.sja.org.uk
www.safe-and-sound.org.uk

CHILDREN WITH SPECIAL NEEDS

Contact a Family
Provides information, advice and support to families of disabled children.
www.cafamily.org.uk

'Waving not drowning' Network
A network of parents of disabled children who work or want to

work. It is run by Working Families, who have various useful factsheets and information available free of charge on parents' rights, flexible working options, etc.
Waving not drowning helpline: 0207 253 7243 (Wed., Thur., Fri.)
Working Families helpline 0800 013 0313 (Mon.–Fri.)
www.workingfamilies.org.uk

Disabled Information and Advice Line (DIAL UK)
National network of advice agencies for people with disabilities. You can download useful factsheets from the DIAL website.
www.dialuk.info

AdviceNow
An independent not-for-profit website run by the Advice Services Alliance, which provides accurate, up-to-date information on rights and legal issues. The AdviceNow information service brings together information on the law and rights from more than 200 UK websites. AdviceNow also has many other useful references on benefits, childcare and tax credits, as well as on a large range of other topics.
www.advicenow.org.uk

Disability Alliance
Provides information and advice on benefits and on financial support for disabled people.
www.disabilityalliance.org

National Childminding Association (NCMA)
For information on childminding and finding childminders. Provides support and resources to childminders, including to work with children with disabilities and special needs.
Helpline: 0800 169 4486
www.ncma.org.uk

Early Support Programme
Aims to ensure that families of disabled children under three receive effective support. You can get more information at www.earlysupport.org.uk and you can order an Early Support Family Pack on 0845 60 222 60.

Pre-school Learning Alliance
For information on preschools and playgroups. Has information and support materials on disability and special educational needs for preschools.
www.pre-school.org.uk

4Children
Provides support for children's service providers, in particular out-of-school clubs.
www.4children.org.uk

Kidsactive
Play and opportunity for disabled children.
www.kidsactive.org.uk

CHILDCARE PUBLICATIONS

The Lady
www.lady.co.uk

Families Online
www.familiesonline.co.uk

TNT
www.tntmagazine.com

Nursery World
www.nurseryworld.co.uk

Simply Childcare
www.simplychildcare.com

ORGANISATIONS FOR PARENTS

National Childbirth Trust
www.nctpregnancyandbabycare.com

Mumsnet
Networking and general information site for mothers.
www.mumsnet.com

Netmums
Networking and general information site for mothers.
www.netmums.com

Working Families (formerly Parents at Work)
Includes legal advice for working parents.
www.workingfamilies.org.uk

Mother at Work
www.motheratwork.co.uk

Nanny Success
www.nannysuccess.com

Index

after-school clubs 23, 27, 240–1
ages of children and childcare options 24, 26–7, 28–9
annualised hours (flexible working) 16
arranging childcare
  how far ahead to start looking 30
  where to start looking 30
au pair plus 26, 146, 157
au pairs 23, 26, 145–80
  accommodation 151
  agencies 162–4
  arrival and showing around 164–6
  au pair plus 26, 146, 157
  babysitting 172–80
  cars and driving 153–4
  costs 157–9
  definitions of an au pair 145–6
  differences from a live-in nanny 150–1
  duties 148–50
  establishing a good relationship 166–8
  free time 154–5
  healthcare 160
  hidden extra costs 158–9
  holiday entitlement 154
  holiday pay 154
  information for a new au pair 165–6
  insurance 160
  mother's help 146, 157–8
  nationality 152
  pros and cons 159–60
  qualifications 156–7
  social life 154–5
  studying 153
  tips to help avoid problems 169–70
  travel to and from the UK 161
  types of au pair 146
  visas 152
  when things go wrong 168–71
  when this may be a good option 147

where to find an au pair 161–4

babysitters 27, 172–80
age limit 173
cancellations 176–7
choosing a babysitter 173
deciding if you can leave your child alone 172–3
definition of babysitting 172
entertainment 177
how to get the most from your babysitter 176–80
information to give to babysitters 177–9
notice 176–7
payment 176
planning ahead 176–7
qualifications 173
refreshments 177
safety issues 177–9
where to find a babysitter 173–6
babysitting service from nurseries 204–5
before-school clubs 23, 27, 240
birth doulas 49
breakfast clubs 23, 27, 240

CACHE diploma 65
child settling in to childcare 30–1
childcare
help in the early days 41–60
mothers who don't work 6
reasons for decision not to use 2–3
childcare barriers and solutions 2–5, 36–40
costs of childcare 4–5, 38–9
guilt 37–8
low self-esteem 39–40
media pressures on mothers 37–8
pressure to stay at home 36
social pressure 36
childcare choice considerations 21–40
ages of children 24, 26–7
arrangements as children grow up 28–9
at-a-glance guide 26–7
basic childcare options 22–8
cost 24, 26–7
full-time or part-time 24, 26–7
home-based or outside the home 28
hours 24, 26–7
live-in or -out 24, 26–7
permanent help when you go back to work 23
registration/inspection 24, 26–7
school-age children 28–9
temporary help at home in the early days 23
year-round care 24, 26–7
childcare plan 31–5
childcare-voucher scheme 17–18, 73, 75, 257
childminders 23, 27, 181–201
advice for avoiding disputes 200
ages covered 186–7

contracts 196–7
costs 186
duties 184–5
hours 186
how to find a registered childminder 190
interviewing a childminder 191–4
keeping a good relationship 198–9
list the things you are looking for 190
making sure your child will fit in 195
meeting your childminder 191–4
myths and reality 182–3
National Childminding Association (NCMA) 181–2
parents' experiences and tips 269–71, 278–9, 274–6
playdates 185
pros and cons 187–8
qualifications 185
questions to ask your childminder 192–4
references 196
registration 181, 185
self-employed status 181
settling in 198
special needs 194–5
typical day 188–9
what to do if there's a problem 199–200
when this may be a good option 182
children with special needs 93–4, 194–5, 203, 224–6, 245–6
children's centres 23, 27, 221–7
children with special needs 224–6
definition and aims 221–2
how to find a children's centre 224
policy and implementation 223
services provided 222
special educational needs coordinator (SENCo) 225–6
Sure Start children's centres 223
when this may be a good option 222–3
compressed hours (flexible working) 16
cost of childcare 4–5, 24, 26–7, 38–9
childcare-voucher scheme 17–18, 73, 75, 257
government help 17–18
help with 17–18
tax credits 17, 257
see also specific types of childcare
CRB disclosure (police check) 73, 74

day nurseries 23, 27, 203–27
children's centres 221–7
children's views on 216
cost 205, 208, 209
definition of a day nursery 203

finding a day nursery 209–10
inspection reports 215
myths and reality 204–6
National Day Nurseries Association (NDNA) 212, 216–17
Ofsted registration and inspection 203, 215
parents' experiences and tips 266–8, 272–3, 276–7
preparing your child for nursery 217–18
problems and complaints 219
pros and cons 207–8
qualifications and staffing 206–7
quality assurance accreditation 216–17
questions to ask on a visit 211–13
references 215
registration 203, 215
settling in to a new nursery 218–19
special educational needs coordinator (SENCo) 203
turnover of staff 205
typical day 208
visiting a nursery 210–13
what you will find in a great nursery 213–15
when this may be a good option 204
workplace nurseries and crèches 220–1
dismissal while on maternity leave 14–15
doulas 23, 26, 47–51
birth doulas 49
cost 49
duties 48
hours 49
interviewing 51
pros and cons 49–50
qualifications 48–9
role of the doula 47
when this may be a good option 48
where to find 50

Early Years Foundation Stage (EYFS) curriculum 229–30, 234–6
emergency childcare 66–7
employer *see* work
extended-schools programme 240

flexi-time 16
flexible working 15–17
full-time or part-time childcare 24, 26–7

government help towards childcare costs 17–18
grandparents *see* relatives looking after children
guilt about using childcare 37–8

holiday clubs 23
holiday play schemes 242
home-based or outside childcare 28

homework clubs 240–1
homeworking 17, 18
hours when childcare is required 24, 26–7
HR department at work, request for flexible working 18–19

inspection of childcare 24, 26–7

jobsharing 16

kindergartens *see* nursery schools

live-in or -out childcare 24, 26–7
low self-esteem in mothers 39–40

male childcarers 67–8
mannies (male nannies) 67–8
maternity leave
  decision to go back to work 11–13
  dismissal during 14–15
  incentives to return early to work 12–13
  pay-rise entitlement 15
  planning your return to work 13–19
  telling your employer when you are coming back 14
  telling your employer you are not coming back 13–14
  unfair dismissal 14–15
maternity nurses 23, 26, 42–7
  booking ahead of time 42, 44
  cost 44
  duties 43
  hours 44
  interviewing 46–7
  pros and cons 45
  qualifications 44
  role of the maternity nurse 42
  when this may be a good option 42–3
  where to find 45
media pressures on mothers 37–8
Montessori nurseries 23, 27, 268
mother's help 23, 26, 55–9
  cost 56
  duties 56
  hours 56–7
  interviewing 59
  pros and cons 57
  qualifications 56
  role of the mother's help 55
  when this may be a good option 55
  where to find 58

nannies 23, 26, 61–122
  advertising for a nanny yourself 85–6
  agencies 82–5
  ages covered 65
  anti-discrimination legislation 92–3
  bank holidays 110

CACHE diploma 65
changes in the family set-up 118–19
checking references 95–101
childcare voucher scheme 73, 75
children with special needs 93–4
choosing candidates to interview 87–9
confidentiality of references 101
contract of employment 107
contractual rights and obligations 107–8
cost 71–3
CRB disclosure (police check) 73, 74
daily (live-out) nanny 63–4
death in the family 118–19
deciding if a nanny is the right option 69
differences from a childminder 62
differences from a mother's help 61–2
differences from a nursery 63
difficulties in the employer-nanny relationship 113–19
divorce and remarriage in the family 118
duties 70–1
emergency childcare 66–7
father's role 116–18
finding a nanny 79–87
first aid certificate 73, 74
guidance on dealing with nanny problems 114–15
handover period for a new nanny 102–4
health problems (nanny) 115
health problems (parent) 115–16
holiday entitlement 95, 110
holiday pay 110
hours 75
induction checklist 102–4
insurance 109
interviewing candidates 89–95
keeping your nanny happy 110–13
live-in or live-out 63–64
male childcarers 67–8
mannies (male nannies) 67–8
maternity rights and pay 109–10
myths and reality 69–70
nanny's diary 78–9
National Insurance contributions 71–3, 109
net salary payment 71–3, 108–10
networking for a nanny 87
new babies 118
new nanny induction 102–4
Norland nannies 69–70
Ofsted Childcare Register (OCR) 73–5
paid holidays 110
parents' experiences and tips 265–6, 269, 271–2, 273–6, 277
pay 71–3, 108–10

permanent nanny 65–6
personality 80
probationary period 95
pros and cons 76–7
public liability insurance 73
qualifications 65, 71, 73–5
reference checking 95–101
registered nannies 73–5
registration procedure 74–5
role of a nanny 61
salary 71–3, 108–10
shared-charge issues 104–6
sick pay 95, 109–10
sole-charge issues 104–6
standard of English required 86
statutory employment rights 107
tax payments (HMRC PAYE) 71–3, 109
temporary nanny 65–6
terminating the nanny-employer relationship 119–21
types of nanny 63–5
typical day 77–9
visitors with children 116
your requirements 79–82
your responsibilities as an employer 106–10
see also nannyshares; night nannies
nannyshares 23, 26, 64–5, 123–43
contractual issues 134
cost benefits 123–4
discipline 128–9
expenses 135–6
feeding and sleeping routines 128
financial issues 134–6
finding a family to share with 125–31
finding the right nanny 131
future plans of both families 127–8
holidays 130
how it works 123–4
interviewing your nanny 132–4
nannies with own children 138–42
National Insurance contributions 134
parents' experiences and tips 263–6
practicalities 124–5
pros and cons 136–7
salaries 135
share location 129–30
shared childcare ethos 127
sharing the costs 135–6
sickness 130–1
sole and shared charge issues 127–8
tax 134
timing and planning 127
treats and trips 129
National Childminding Association (NCMA) 181–2
National Day Nurseries Association (NDNA) 212, 216–17
new baby, help in the early days 41–60

night nannies 23, 26, 51–5
  cost 53
  duties 52
  hours 53
  interviewing 54–5
  pros and cons 53
  qualifications 52
  role of the night nanny 51
  when this may be a good option 52
  where to find 54
nurseries *see* day nurseries; nursery schools
nursery schools 27, 229–47
  ages covered 230
  children with special needs 245–6
  choosing a nursery school 233–4
  comparison with playgroups 238
  costs 232
  curriculum 229–30, 234–6
  Early Years Foundation Stage (EYFS) curriculum 229–30, 234–6
  eligibility for a free early-learning place 232
  Foundation Stage Profile 236
  free early-learning entitlement 232
  inspection 229
  preparing your child for nursery school 236–7
  pros and cons 231
  questions to ask 233–4
  registration 229
  services offered 229
  staff ratio 230
  timetable 230
  what to expect from a nursery school 234–6
  your child's progress 236

Ofsted Childcare Register (OCR) 73–5
Ofsted inspection 25, 26–7

parent-and-toddler groups 239
parental leave from work 15
parents' experiences and top tips 263–79
part-time working 15–17
pay-rise entitlement during maternity leave 15
playgroups 27, 238–9
  advantages 239
  ages covered 239
  children with special needs 245–6
  comparison with nursery schools 238–9
  Ofsted registration 238
police check (CRB disclosure) 73, 74
pre-schools *see* nursery schools

registration of childcare 24, 26–7
relatives looking after children 23, 26, 249–62
  benefits of grandparents' involvement 249–50
  common choices of relations 250
  costs 251, 256–7

finding diplomatic solutions to problems 259–60
good communication 256
Grandparents' Charter 253
ground rules 255–6
increase in use of informal care 249
maintaining good 'relations' 259–60
making relative care work 252–60
personal family issues 258
problems which may arise 260–1
pros and cons 251
realistic assessment of the situation 253–4
remuneration 256–7
sources of information and support 258
tax break eligibility 257
voucher scheme eligibility 257
when it is time for a change 260–1
when this may be a good option 250–1
written agreement 254–5

school-age children 28–9
school-based care 239–47
after-school clubs 23, 27, 240–1
benefits of extended schools 242–3
breakfast clubs 23, 27, 240
children with special needs 245–6
costs 245
extended-schools programme 240
holiday play schemes 242
homework clubs 240–1
pros and cons 243–4
schools working in partnerships 243
wraparound care 23, 27, 241–2
self-esteem of mothers, returning to work 39–40
sessional care 23
settling a child into childcare 30–1
social pressure to be a stay-at-home mother 36
special needs 93–4, 194–5, 203, 224–6, 245–6
special educational needs coordinator (SENCo) 203, 225–6
staggered hours (flexible working) 16
Sure Start children's centres 223

tax credits 17, 257
tax payments *see specific types of childcare*

unfair dismissal 14–15

voucher scheme for childcare 17–18, 73, 75, 257

work
barriers to going back 2–5

childcare backup scheme 66–7
decision to go back to work 11–13
dismissal while on maternity leave 14–15
emergency childcare 66–7
flexible working 15–17
flexible working request 18–19
guilt about using childcare 37–8
help with financing childcare 17–18
homeworking 17, 18
incentives to return early 12–13
parental leave 15
part-time working 15–17
pay-rise entitlement during maternity leave 15
planning your return to work 13–19
self-esteem when returning 39–40
support for working parents 18–19
talking to the HR department 18–19
telling your employer when you are coming back 14
telling your employer you are not coming back 13–14
unfair dismissal 14–15
workplace nurseries and crèches 23, 27, 220–1
wraparound care 23, 27, 241–2

year-round childcare 24, 26–7